Plato's Beauty
harmony
continuity
order
Truth?
Good?

artist
concentrated Beauty
in the sensuos.

ART

Hegel's Philosophy
manifestation of the absolute spirit

LOGIC   Nature   Spirit
                                   art, religion, philos.

THESIS – ART   Being
ANTITHESIS- Religion Non-being
Synthesis - philos   becoming

ORIENTAL ART
CLASSICAL
Romantic (intellectual)

significant form is Beauty

Beauty is truth

Bk. Arts, Artist & Art Education.
Kenneth M. Lansing.
Philosophies
of Art & Beauty

Reserving Chap 6

ART

BY CLIVE BELL

CAPRICORN BOOKS
NEW YORK

Reprinted by arrangement with Chatto & Windus Ltd.

Capricorn Books, G. P. Putnam's Sons, New York, 1958

TENTH IMPRESSION

SBN: 399-50027-8

Library of Congress Catalog
Card Number: 58-59755

MANUFACTURED IN THE UNITED STATES OF AMERICA

CONTENTS

PREFACE

IN this little book I have tried to develop a complete theory of visual art. I have put forward an hypothesis by reference to which the respectability, though not the validity, of all aesthetic judgments can be tested, in the light of which the history of art from paleolithic days to the present becomes intelligible, by adopting which we give intellectual backing to an almost universal and immemorial conviction. Everyone in his heart believes that there is a real distinction between works of art and all other objects; this belief my hypothesis justifies. We all feel that art is immensely important; my hypothesis affords reason for thinking it so. In fact, the great merit of this hypothesis of mine is that it seems to explain what we know to be true. Anyone who is curious to discover why we call a Persian carpet or a fresco by Piero della Francesca a work of art, and a portrait-bust of Hadrian or a popular problem-picture rubbish, will here find satisfaction. He will find, too, that to the familiar counters of criticism—*e.g.* "good drawing," "magnificent design," "mechanical," "unfelt," "ill-organised," "sensitive,"—is given, what such terms sometimes lack, a definite meaning. In a word, my hypothesis works; that is unusual: to some it has seemed not only workable but true; that is miraculous almost.

In fifty or sixty thousand words, though one may develop a theory adequately, one cannot pretend to develop it exhaustively. My book is a simplification. I have tried to make a generalisation about the nature of art that shall be at once true, coherent, and comprehensible. I have sought a theory which should explain the whole of my aesthetic experience and suggest a solution of every problem, but I have not attempted to answer in detail all the questions that proposed themselves, or to follow any one of them

along its slenderest ramifications. The science of aesthetics
is a complex business and so is the history of art; my hope
has been to write about them something simple and true.
For instance, though I have indicated very clearly, and
even repetitiously, what I take to be essential in a work of
art, I have not discussed as fully as I might have done the
relation of the essential to the unessential. There is a great
deal more to be said about the mind of the artist and the
nature of the artistic problem. It remains for someone
who is an artist, a psychologist, and an expert in human
limitations to tell us how far the unessential is a necessary
means to the essential—to tell us whether it is easy or
difficult or impossible for the artist to destroy every rung
in the ladder by which he has climbed to the stars.

My first chapter epitomises discussions and conversations
and long strands of cloudy speculation which, condensed
to solid argument, would still fill two or three stout volumes: some day, perhaps, I shall write one of them if my
critics are rash enough to provoke me. As for my third
chapter—a sketch of the history of fourteen hundred years
—that it is a simplification goes without saying. Here I
have used a series of historical generalisations to illustrate
my theory; and here, again, I believe in my theory, and
am persuaded that anyone who will consider the history of
art in its light will find that history more intelligible than
of old. At the same time I willingly admit that in fact the
contrasts are less violent, the hills less precipitous, than
they must be made to appear in a chart of this sort. Doubtless it would be well if this chapter also were expanded
into half a dozen readable volumes, but that it cannot be
until the learned authorities have learnt to write or some
writer has learnt to be patient.

Those conversations and discussions that have tempered
and burnished the theories advanced in my first chapter
have been carried on for the most part with Mr. Roger Fry,
to whom, therefore, I owe a debt that defies exact computation. In the first place, I can thank him, as joint-editor of
The Burlington Magazine, for permission to reprint some
part of an essay contributed by me to that periodical. That

obligation discharged, I come to a more complicated reck-
oning. The first time I met Mr. Fry, in a railway carriage
plying between Cambridge and London, we fell into talk
about contemporary art and its relation to all other art; it
seems to me sometimes that we have been talking about
the same thing ever since, but my friends assure me that
it is not quite so bad as that. Mr. Fry, I remember, had
recently become familiar with the modern French masters
—Cézanne, Gauguin, Matisse: I enjoyed the advantage of
a longer acquaintance. Already, however, Mr. Fry had
published his *Essay in Aesthetics,* which, to my thinking,
was the most helpful contribution to the science that had
been made since the days of Kant. We talked a good deal
about that essay, and then we discussed the possibility of
a "Post-Impressionist" Exhibition at the Grafton Galleries.
We did not call it "Post-Impressionist"; the word was invented later by Mr. Fry, which makes me think it a little
hard that the more advanced critics should so often up-
braid him for not knowing what "Post-Impressionism"
means.

For some years Mr. Fry and I have been arguing, more
or less amicably, about the principles of aesthetics. We still
disagree profoundly. I like to think that I have not moved
an inch from my original position, but I must confess that
the cautious doubts and reservations that have insinuated
themselves into this Preface are all indirect consequences
of my friend's criticism. And it is not only of general ideas
and fundamental things that we have talked; Mr. Fry and
I have wrangled for hours about particular works of art.
In such cases the extent to which one may have affected the
judgment of the other cannot possibly be appraised, nor
need it be: neither of us, I think, covets the doubtful hon-
ours of proselytism. Surely whoever appreciates a fine work
of art may be allowed the exquisite pleasure of supposing
that he has made a discovery? Nevertheless, since all artistic theories are based on aesthetic judgments, it is clear
that should one affect the judgments of another, he may
affect, indirectly, some of his theories; and it is certain that
some of my historical generalisations have been modified,

and even demolished, by Mr. Fry. His task was not arduous: he had merely to confront me with some work over which he was sure that I should go into ecstasies, and then to prove by the most odious and irrefragable evidence that it belonged to a period which I had concluded, on the highest *a priori* grounds, to be utterly barren. I can only hope that Mr. Fry's scholarship has been as profitable to me as it has been painful: I have travelled with him through France, Italy, and the near East, suffering acutely, not always, I am glad to remember, in silence; for the man who stabs a generalisation with a fact forfeits all claim on good-fellowship and the usages of polite society.

I have to thank my friend Mr. Vernon Rendall for permission to make what use I chose of the articles I have contributed from time to time to *The Athenaeum:* if I have made any use of what belongs by law to the proprietors of other papers I herewith offer the customary dues. My readers will be as grateful as I to M. Vignier, M. Druet, and Mr. Kevorkian, of the Persian Art Gallery, since it is they who have made it certain that the purchaser will get something he likes for his money. To Mr. Eric Maclagan of South Kensington, and Mr. Joyce of the British Museum, I owe a more private and particular debt. My wife has been good enough to read both the MS. and proof of this book; she has corrected some errors, and called attention to the more glaring offences against Christian charity. You must not attempt, therefore, to excuse the author on the ground of inadvertence or haste.

CLIVE BELL

November 1913

PREFACE TO NEW EDITION

To bring *Art* up to date, that is to make what I thought and felt in 1911 and 1912 square with what I think and feel to-day, would be to write a new book. That I shall not do: for one thing because I am lazy; for another because, if *Art* has any value for future generations it will be as a record of what people like myself were thinking and feeling in the years before the first War. So let exaggerations, childish simplifications and injustices stand.

Some errors have been rectified in this or earlier editions; of these the most surprising—one that survived for years in numerous editions produced in this country and America—was the printing of "Gaugin" for Gauguin. It is surely to the credit of reviewers of my generation, many of whom were not much in love with my ideas, that not one thought fit to reproach me with this misprint—except Professor Tonks who was not a reviewer. Whether it was magnanimity that prevented them espying a gross tautology in my statement of the aesthetic hypothesis I cannot be sure: this stain, I may say, was obliterated long ago. To the best of my belief I have never been taken to task for a sentence (it is still there) which ranks Seurat slightingly with Signac and Cross. For this judgment my only excuse was that I had seen very little of the master's work, and that, of course, is no excuse for anyone who has taken it on himself to favour the public with his views. On the other hand, I would like to make some apology for a denigratory note which, in another book, *Landmarks in Nineteenth Century Painting*, I let fly at Degas. Degas was a great, a very great, artist; but I had been exasperated by a fashion, at one time prevalent amongst English people who knew very little of French painting, of belauding the Beach Scene in the Tate at the expense of better pictures.

La Plage is far from being one of Degas' masterpieces; but it is brilliant, and brilliant in a way that can be easily appreciated. I was indignant, and, as generally happens when one is in that exalted state, said something silly.

These are particular blemishes; the more general faults of this book are not altogether unbecoming to youth. The tone is too confident and too pugnacious. A whiff of propaganda emanates from pages where propaganda is out of place; but you must remember that "the battle of Post-Impressionism" had just been joined. The best that even Sickert would say for Cézanne, in 1911, was that he was "un grand raté," while Sargent called him a "botcher," and the director of the Tate Gallery refused to hang his pictures. Van Gogh was denounced every day almost as an incompetent and vulgar madman; M. Jacques-Emile Blanche informed us that, when cleaning his palette, he often produced something better than a Gauguin; and when Roger Fry showed a Matisse to the Art-Workers Guild the cry went up "drink or drugs?" To lose one's temper with "Art-Workers" or a Slade professor may be silly, but do not forget that honoured artists and critics— to say nothing of novelists, poets, judges, bishops, politicians and biologists—joined in the cry. Hark to Sickert: "Matisse has all the worst art-school tricks" . . . "Picasso, like all Whistler's followers, has annexed Whistler's empty background without annexing the one quality by which Whistler made his empty background interesting." Perhaps we did well to be angry. Nevertheless, anyone who reads this book will see that, being angry, I speak absurdly and impertinently of the giants of the High Renaissance, that I under-rate the eighteenth century, and that I think it necessary, for ridiculous doctrinaire reasons, to qualify my admiration for the Impressionists. The tone of the book, as I said, is too confident besides being aggressive. The generalisations are too sweeping; the history of fourteen hundred years, which is told in seventy-five pages, is told, not as it should be told if it is to be told so briefly, in black and white, but in violently contrasted colours: also some of the colours are false. Besides all this, there is a deal of optimism which has been made to look funny by the events of the last thirty-five years; but then events were not under the author's control. And yet, re-reading *Art,* and taking into account all, but I think no more than all, the extenuating circumstances that may be urged in its defence, I cannot but feel a little envious of the adventurous young man who wrote it.

                                                          CLIVE BELL

CHARLESTON, *October* 1948

I

WHAT IS ART?

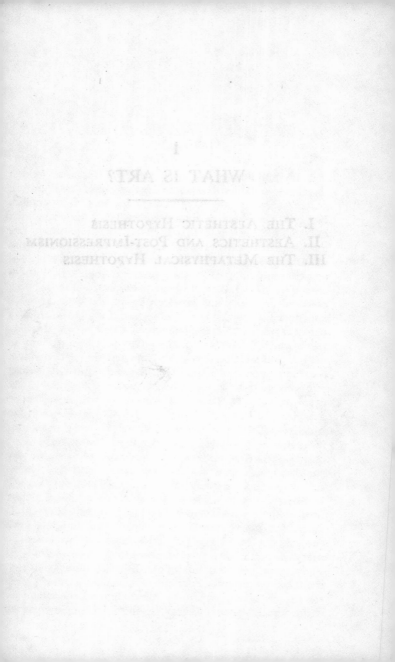

1. THE AESTHETIC HYPOTHESIS

IT IS improbable that more nonsense has been written about aesthetics than about anything else: the literature of the subject is not large enough for that. It is certain, however, that about no subject with which I am acquainted has so little been said that is at all to the purpose. The explanation is discoverable. He who would elaborate a plausible theory of aesthetics must possess two qualities—artistic sensibility and a turn for clear thinking. Without sensibility a man can have no aesthetic experience, and, obviously, theories not based on broad and deep aesthetic experience are worthless. Only those for whom art is a constant source of passionate emotion can possess the data from which profitable theories may be deduced; but to deduce profitable theories even from accurate data involves a certain amount of brain-work, and, unfortunately, robust intellects and delicate sensibilities are not inseparable. As often as not, the hardest thinkers have had no aesthetic experience whatever. I have a friend blessed with an intellect as keen as a drill, who, though he takes an interest in aesthetics, has never during a life of almost forty years been guilty of an aesthetic emotion. So, having no faculty for distinguishing a work of art from a handsaw, he is apt to rear up a pyramid of irrefragable argument on the hypothesis that a handsaw is a work of art. This defect robs his perspicuous and subtle reasoning of much of its value; for it has ever been a maxim that faultless logic can win but little credit for conclusions that are based on premises notoriously false. Every cloud, however, has its silver lining, and this insensibility, though unlucky in that it makes my friend incapable of choosing a sound basis for his argument, mercifully blinds him to the absurdity of his conclusions while leaving him in full enjoyment of his masterly dialectic. People who set out from the hypothesis that Sir Edwin Landseer was the finest painter that ever lived will feel no uneasiness about an aesthetic which proves that Giotto was the worst. So, my friend, when he arrives very logically at the conclusion that a work of art should be small or round or smooth, or that to appreciate fully a picture you should pace smartly before it or set it spinning like a top, cannot guess why I ask him whether he has lately been to Cambridge, a place he sometimes visits.

On the other hand, people who respond immediately and surely to works of art, though, in my judgment, more enviable than men of massive intellect but slight sensibility, are often quite as incapable of talking sense about aesthetics. Their heads are not always very clear. They possess the data on which any system must be based; but, generally, they want the power that draws correct inferences from true data. Having received aesthetic emotions from works of art, they are in a position to seek out the quality common to all that have moved them, but, in fact, they do nothing of the sort. I do not blame them. Why should they bother to examine their feelings when for them to feel is enough? Why should they stop to think when they are not very good at thinking? Why should they hunt for a common quality in all objects that move them in a particular way when they can linger over the many delicious and peculiar charms of each as it comes? So, if they write criticism and call it aesthetics, if they imagine that they are talking about Art when they are talking about particular works of art or even about the technique of painting, if loving particular works they find tedious the consideration of art in general, perhaps they have chosen the better part. If they are not curious about the nature of their emotion, nor about the quality common to all objects that provoke it, they have my sympathy, and, as what they say is often charming and suggestive, my admiration too. Only let no one suppose that what they write and talk is aesthetics; it is criticism, or just "shop."

The starting-point for all systems of aesthetics must be

the personal experience of a peculiar emotion. The objects that provoke this emotion we call works of art. All sensitive people agree that there is a peculiar emotion provoked by works of art. I do not mean, of course, that all works provoke the same emotion. On the contrary, every work produces a different emotion. But all these emotions are recognisably the same in kind; so far, at any rate, the best opinion is on my side. That there is a particular kind of emotion provoked by works of visual art, and that this emotion is provoked by every kind of visual art, by pictures, sculptures, buildings, pots, carvings, textiles, &c., &c., is not disputed, I think, by anyone capable of feeling it. This emotion is called the aesthetic emotion; and if we can discover some quality common and peculiar to all the objects that provoke it, we shall have solved what I take to be the central problem of aesthetics. We shall have discovered the essential quality in a work of art, the quality that distinguishes works of art from all other classes of objects.

For either all works of visual art have some common quality, or when we speak of "works of art" we gibber. Everyone speaks of "art," making a mental classification by which he distinguishes the class "works of art" from all other classes. What is the justification of this classification? What is the quality common and peculiar to all members of this class? Whatever it be, no doubt it is often found in company with other qualities; but they are adventitious —it is essential. There must be some one quality without which a work of art cannot exist; possessing which, in the least degree, no work is altogether worthless. What is this quality? What quality is shared by all objects that provoke our aesthetic emotions? What quality is common to Sta. Sophia and the windows at Chartres, Mexican sculpture, a Persian bowl, Chinese carpets, Giotto's frescoes at Padua, and the masterpieces of Poussin, Piero della Francesca, and Cézanne? Only one answer seems possible —significant form. In each, lines and colours combined in a particular way, certain forms and relations of forms, stir our aesthetic emotions. These relations and combinations of lines and colours, these aesthetically moving forms, I call "Significant Form"; and "Significant Form" is the one quality common to all works of visual art.

At this point it may be objected that I am making aesthetics a purely subjective business, since my only data are personal experiences of a particular emotion. It will be said that the objects that provoke this emotion vary with each individual, and that therefore a system of aesthetics can have no objective validity. It must be replied that any system of aesthetics which pretends to be based on some objective truth is so palpably ridiculous as not to be worth discussing. We have no other means of recognising a work of art than our feeling for it. The objects that provoke aesthetic emotion vary with each individual. Aesthetic judgments are, as the saying goes, matters of taste; and about tastes, as everyone is proud to admit, there is no disputing. A good critic may be able to make me see in a picture that had left me cold things that I had overlooked, till at last, receiving the aesthetic emotion, I recognise it as a work of art. To be continually pointing out those parts, the sum, or rather the combination, of which unite to produce significant form, is the function of criticism. But it is useless for a critic to tell me that something is a work of art; he must make me feel it for myself. This he can do only by making me see; he must get at my emotions through my eyes. Unless he can make me see something that moves me, he cannot force my emotions. I have no right to consider anything a work of art to which I cannot react emotionally; and I have no right to look for the essential quality in anything that I have not *felt* to be a work of art. The critic can affect my aesthetic theories only by affecting my aesthetic experience. All systems of aesthetics must be based on personal experience—that is to say, they must be subjective.

Yet, though all aesthetic theories must be based on aesthetic judgments, and ultimately all aesthetic judgments must be matters of personal taste, it would be rash to assert that no theory of aesthetics can have general validity. For, though A, B, C, D are the works that move me, and

A, D, E, F the works that move you, it may well be that x is the only quality believed by either of us to be common to all the works in his list. We may all agree about aesthetics, and yet differ about particular works of art. We may differ as to the presence or absence of the quality x. My immediate object will be to show that significant form is the only quality common and peculiar to all the works of visual art that move me; and I will ask those whose aesthetic experience does not tally with mine to see whether this quality is not also, in their judgment, common to all works that move them, and whether they can discover any other quality of which the same can be said.

Also at this point a query arises, irrelevant indeed, but hardly to be suppressed: "Why are we so profoundly moved by forms related in a particular way?" The question is extremely interesting, but irrelevant to aesthetics. In pure aesthetics we have only to consider our emotion and its object: for the purposes of aesthetics we have no right, neither is there any necessity, to pry behind the object into the state of mind of him who made it. Later, I shall attempt to answer the question; for by so doing I may be able to develop my theory of the relation of art to life. I shall not, however, be under the delusion that I am rounding off my theory of aesthetics. For a discussion of aesthetics, it need be agreed only that forms arranged and combined according to certain unknown and mysterious laws do move us in a particular way, and that it is the business of an artist so to combine and arrange them that they shall move us. These moving combinations and arrangements I have called, for the sake of convenience and for a reason that will appear later, "Significant Form."

A third interruption has to be met.

"Are you forgetting about colour?" someone inquires. Certainly not; my term "significant form" included combinations of lines and of colours. The distinction between form and colour is an unreal one; you cannot conceive a colourless line or a colourless space; neither can you conceive a formless relation of colours. In a black and white drawing the spaces are all white and all are bounded by black lines;

in most oil paintings the spaces are multi-coloured and so
are the boundaries; you cannot imagine a boundary line
without any content, or a content without a boundary line.
Therefore, when I speak of significant form, I mean a
combination of lines and colours (counting white and black
as colours) that moves me aesthetically.

Some people may be surprised at my not having called
this "beauty." Of course, to those who define beauty as
"combinations of lines and colours that provoke aesthetic
emotion," I willingly concede the right of substituting their
word for mine. But most of us, however strict we may be,
are apt to apply the epithet "beautiful" to objects that do
not provoke that peculiar emotion produced by works of
art. Everyone, I suspect, has called a butterfly or a flower
beautiful. Does anyone feel the same kind of emotion for a
butterfly or a flower that he feels for a cathedral or a
picture? Surely, it is not what I call an aesthetic emotion
that most of us feel, generally, for natural beauty. I shall
suggest, later, that some people may, occasionally, see in
nature what we see in art, and feel for her an aesthetic
emotion; but I am satisfied that, as a rule, most people feel
a very different kind of emotion for birds and flowers and
the wings of butterflies from that which they feel for
pictures, pots, temples and statues. Why these beautiful
things do not move us as works of art move is another,
and not an aesthetic, question. For our immediate purpose
we have to discover only what quality is common to objects
that do move us as works of art. In the last part of this
chapter, when I try to answer the question—"Why are we
so profoundly moved by some combinations of lines and
colours?" I shall hope to offer an acceptable explanation
of why we are less profoundly moved by others.

Since we call a quality that does not raise the characteristic aesthetic emotion "Beauty," it would be misleading
to call by the same name the quality that does. To make
"beauty" the object of the aesthetic emotion, we must give
to the word an over-strict and unfamiliar definition. Everyone sometimes uses "beauty" in an unaesthetic sense; most
people habitually do so. To everyone, except perhaps here

and there an occasional aesthete, the commonest sense of the word is unaesthetic. Of its grosser abuse, patent in our chatter about "beautiful huntin'" and "beautiful shootin'," I need not take account; it would be open to the precious to reply that they never do so abuse it. Besides, here there is no danger of confusion between the aesthetic and the non-aesthetic use; but when we speak of a beautiful woman there is. When an ordinary man speaks of a beautiful woman he certainly does not mean only that she moves him aesthetically; but when an artist calls a withered old hag beautiful he may sometimes mean what he means when he calls a battered torso beautiful. The ordinary man, if he be also a man of taste, will call the battered torso beautiful, but he will not call a withered hag beautiful because, in the matter of women, it is not to the aesthetic quality that the hag may possess, but to some other quality that he assigns the epithet. Indeed, most of us never dream of going for aesthetic emotions to human beings, from whom we ask something very different. This "something," when we find it in a young woman, we are apt to call "beauty." We live in a nice age. With the man-in-the-street "beautiful" is more often than not synonymous with "desirable"; the word does not necessarily connote any aesthetic reaction whatever, and I am tempted to believe that in the minds of many the sexual flavour of the word is stronger than the aesthetic. I have noticed a consistency in those to whom the most beautiful thing in the world is a beautiful woman, and the next most beautiful thing a picture of one. The confusion between aesthetic and sensual beauty is not in their case so great as might be supposed. Perhaps there is none; for perhaps they have never had an aesthetic emotion to confuse with their other emotions. The art that they call "beautiful" is generally closely related to the women. A beautiful picture is a photograph of a pretty girl; beautiful music, the music that provokes emotions similar to those provoked by young ladies in musical farces; and beautiful poetry, the poetry that recalls the same emotions felt, twenty years earlier, for the rector's daughter. Clearly the word "beauty" is used to connote the objects of quite

distinguishable emotions, and that is a reason for not employing a term which would land me inevitably in con-
fusions and misunderstandings with my readers.

On the other hand, with those who judge it more exact
to call these combinations and arrangements of form that
provoke our aesthetic emotions, not "significant form," but
"significant relations of form," and then try to make the
best of two worlds, the aesthetic and the metaphysical, by
calling these relations "rhythm," I have no quarrel whatever. Having made it clear that by "significant form" I
mean arrangements and combinations that move us in a
particular way, I willingly join hands with those who prefer
to give a different name to the same thing.

The hypothesis that significant form is the essential
quality in a work of art has at least one merit denied to
many more famous and more striking—it does help to
explain things. We are all familiar with pictures that
interest us and excite our admiration, but do not move us
as works of art. To this class belongs what I call "Descriptive Painting"—that is, painting in which forms are used
not as objects of emotion, but as means of suggesting
emotion or conveying information. Portraits of psy-
chological and historical value, topographical works, pictures that tell stories and suggest situations, illustrations of
all sorts, belong to this class. That we all recognize the
distinction is clear, for who has not said that such and such
a drawing was excellent as illustration, but as a work of art
worthless? Of course many descriptive pictures possess,
amongst other qualities, formal significance, and are therefore works of art: but many more do not. They interest us;
they may move us too in a hundred different ways, but
they do not move us aesthetically. According to my hypothesis they are not works of art. They leave untouched our
aesthetic emotions because it is not their forms but the
ideas or information suggested or conveyed by their forms
that affect us.

Few pictures are better known or liked than Frith's
"Paddington Station"; certainly I should be the last to
grudge it its popularity. Many a weary forty minutes have

I whiled away disentangling its fascinating incidents and forging for each an imaginary past and an improbable future. But certain though it is that Frith's masterpiece, or engravings of it, have provided thousands with half-hours of curious and fanciful pleasure, it is not less certain that no one has experienced before it one half-second of aesthetic rapture—and this although the picture contains several pretty passages of colour, and is by no means badly painted. "Paddington Station" is not a work of art; it is an interesting and amusing document. In it line and colour are used to recount anecdotes, suggest ideas, and indicate the manners and customs of an age: they are not used to provoke aesthetic emotion. Forms and the relations of forms were for Frith not objects of emotion, but means of suggesting emotion and conveying ideas.

The ideas and information conveyed by "Paddington Station" are so amusing and so well presented that the picture has considerable value and is well worth preserving. But, with the perfection of photographic processes and of the cinematograph, pictures of this sort are becoming otiose. Who doubts that one of those *Daily Mirror* photographers in collaboration with a *Daily Mail* reporter can tell us far more about "London day by day" than any Royal Academician? For an account of manners and fashions we shall go, in future, to photographs, supported by a little bright journalism, rather than to descriptive painting. Had the imperial academicians of Nero, instead of manufacturing incredibly loathsome imitations of the antique, recorded in fresco and mosaic the manners and fashions of their day, their stuff, though artistic rubbish, would now be an historical gold-mine. If only they had been Friths instead of being Alma Tademas! But photography has made impossible any such transmutation of modern rubbish. Therefore it must be confessed that pictures in the Frith tradition are grown superfluous; they merely waste the hours of able men who might be more profitably employed in works of a wider beneficence. Still, they are not unpleasant, which is more than can be said for that kind of descriptive painting of which "The Doctor" is the most flagrant example. Of course "The Doctor" is not a work of art. In it form is not used as an object of emotion, but as a means of suggesting emotions. This alone suffices to make it nugatory; it is worse than nugatory because the emotion it suggests is false. What it suggests is not pity and admiration but a sense of complacency in our own pitifulness and generosity. It is sentimental. Art is above morals, or, rather, all art is moral because, as I hope to show presently, works of art are immediate means to good. Once we have judged a thing a work of art, we have judged it ethically of the first importance and put it beyond the reach of the moralist. But descriptive pictures which are not works of art, and, therefore, are not necessarily means to good states of mind, are proper objects of the ethical philosopher's attention. Not being a work of art, "The Doctor" has none of the immense ethical value possessed by all objects that provoke aesthetic ecstasy; and the state of mind to which it is a means, as illustration, appears to me undesirable.

The works of those enterprising young men, the Italian Futurists, are notable examples of descriptive painting. Like the Royal Academicians, they use form, not to provoke aesthetic emotions, but to convey information and ideas. Indeed, the published theories of the Futurists prove that their pictures ought to have nothing whatever to do with art. Their social and political theories are respectable, but I would suggest to young Italian painters that it is possible to become a Futurist in thought and action and yet remain an artist, if one has the luck to be born one. To associate art with politics is always a mistake. Futurist pictures are descriptive because they aim at presenting in line and colour the chaos of the mind at a particular moment; their forms are not intended to promote aesthetic emotion but to convey information. These forms, by the way, whatever may be the nature of the ideas they suggest, are themselves anything but revolutionary. In such Futurist pictures as I have seen—perhaps I should except some by Severini— the drawing, whenever it becomes representative as it frequently does, is found to be in that soft and common convention brought into fashion by Besnard some thirty years ago, and much affected by Beaux-Art students ever since. As works of art, the Futurist pictures are negligible; but they are not to be judged as works of art. A good Futurist picture would succeed as a good piece of psychology succeeds; it would reveal, through line and colour, the complexities of an interesting state of mind. If Futurist pictures seem to fail, we must seek an explanation, not in a lack of artistic qualities that they never were intended to possess, but rather in the minds the states of which they are intended to reveal.

Most people who care much about art find that of the work that moves them most the greater part is what scholars call "Primitive." Of course there are bad primitives. For instance, I remember going, full of enthusiasm, to see one of the earliest Romanesque churches in Poitiers (Notre-Dame-la-Grande), and finding it as ill-proportioned, over-decorated, coarse, fat and heavy as any better class building by one of those highly civilised architects who flourished a thousand years earlier or eight hundred later. But such exceptions are rare. As a rule primitive art is good—and here again my hypothesis is helpful—for, as a rule, it is also free from descriptive qualities. In primitive art you will find no accurate representation; you will find only significant form. Yet no other art moves us so profoundly. Whether we consider Sumerian sculpture or predynastic Egyptian art, or archaic Greek, or the Wei and T'ang masterpieces,[1] or those early Japanese works of which I had the luck to see a few superb examples (especially two wooden Bodhisattvas) at the Shepherd's

[1] The existence of the Ku K'ai-chih makes it clear that the art of this period (fifth to eighth centuries), was a typical primitive movement. To call the great vital art of the Liang, Chen, Wei, and Tang dynasties a development out of the exquisitely refined and exhausted art of the Han decadence—from which Ku K'ai-chih is a delicate straggler—is to call Romanesque sculpture a development out of Praxiteles. Between the two something has happened to refill the stream of art. What had happened in China was the spiritual and emotional revolution that followed the onset of Buddhism.

Bush Exhibition in 1910, or whether, coming nearer home, we consider the primitive Byzantine art of the sixth century and its primitive developments amongst the Western barbarians, or, turning far afield, we consider that mysterious and majestic art that flourished in Central and South America before the coming of the white men, in every case we observe three common characteristics—absence of representation, absence of technical swagger, sublimely impressive form. Nor is it hard to discover the connection between these three. Formal significance loses itself in preoccupation with exact representation and ostentatious cunning.[1]

Naturally, it is said that if there is little representation and less saltimbancery in primitive art, that is because the primitives were unable to catch a likeness or cut intellectual capers. The contention is beside the point. There is truth in it, no doubt, though, were I a critic whose reputation depended on a power of impressing the public with a semblance of knowledge, I should be more cautious about urging it than such people generally are. For to suppose that the Byzantine masters wanted skill, or could not have created an illusion had they wished to do so, seems to imply ignorance of the amazingly dexterous realism of the

[1] This is not to say that exact representation is bad in itself. It is indifferent. A perfectly represented form may be significant, only it is fatal to sacrifice significance to representation. The quarrel between significance and illusion seems to be as old as art itself, and I have little doubt that what makes most palaeolithic art so bad is a preoccupation with exact representation. Evidently palaeolithic draughtsmen had no sense of the significance of form. Their art resembles that of the more capable and sincere Royal Academicians: it is a little higher than that of Sir Edward Poynter and a little lower than that of the late Lord Leighton. That this is no paradox let the cave-drawings of Altamira, or such works as the sketches of horses found at Bruniquel and now in the British Museum, bear witness. If the ivory head of a girl from the Grotte du Pape, Brassempouy (*Musée St. Germain*) and the ivory torso found at the same place (*Collection St. Cric*), be, indeed, palaeolithic, then there were good palaeolithic artists who created and did not imitate form. Neolithic art is, of course, a very different matter.

notoriously bad works of that age. Very often, I fear, the misrepresentation of the primitives must be attributed to what the critics call, "wilful distortion." Be that as it may, the point is that, either from want of skill or want of will, primitives neither create illusions, nor make display of extravagant accomplishment, but concentrate their energies on the one thing needful—the creation of form. Thus have they created the finest works of art that we possess.

Let no one imagine that representation is bad in itself; a realistic form may be as significant, in its place as part of the design, as an abstract. But if a representative form has value, it as form, not as representation. The representative element in a work of art may or may not be harmful; always it is irrelevant. For, to appreciate a work of art we need bring with us nothing from life, no knowledge of its ideas and affairs, no familiarity with its emotions. Art transports us from the world of man's activity to a world of aesthetic exaltation. For a moment we are shut off from human interests; our anticipations and memories are arrested; we are lifted above the stream of life. The pure mathematician rapt in his studies knows a state of mind which I take to be similar, if not identical. He feels an emotion for his speculations which arises from no perceived relation between them and the lives of men, but springs, inhuman or super-human, from the heart of an abstract science. I wonder, sometimes, whether the appreciators of art and of mathematical solutions are not even more closely allied. Before we feel an aesthetic emotion for a combination of forms, do we not perceive intellectually the rightness and necessity of the combination? If we do, it would explain the fact that passing rapidly through a room we recognise a picture to be good, although we cannot say that it has provoked much emotion. We seem to have recognised intellectually the rightness of its forms without staying to fix our attention, and collect, as it were, their emotional significance. If this were so, it would be permissible to inquire whether it was the forms themselves or our perception of their rightness and necessity that caused aesthetic emotion. But I do not think I need linger to discuss the matter here. I have been inquiring why certain combinations of forms move us; I should not have travelled by other roads had I enquired, instead, why certain combinations are perceived to be right and necessary, and why our perception of their rightness and necessity is moving. What I have to say is this: the rapt philosopher, and he who contemplates a work of art, inhabit a world with an intense and peculiar significance of its own; that significance is unrelated to the significance of life. In this world the emotions of life find no place. It is a world with emotions of its own.

To appreciate a work of art we need bring with us nothing but a sense of form and colour and a knowledge of three-dimensional space. That bit of knowledge, I admit, is essential to the appreciation of many great works, since many of the most moving forms ever created are in three dimensions. To see a cube or a rhomboid as a flat pattern is to lower its significance, and a sense of three-dimensional space is essential to the full appreciation of most architectural forms. Pictures which would be insignificant if we saw them as flat patterns are profoundly moving because, in fact, we see them as related planes. If the representation of three-dimensional space is to be called "representation," then I agree that there is one kind of representation which is not irrelevant. Also, I agree that along with our feeling for line and colour we must bring with us our knowledge of space if we are to make the most of every kind of form. Nevertheless, there are magnificent designs to an appreciation of which this knowledge is not necessary: so, though it is not irrelevant to the appreciation of some works of art it is not essential to the appreciation of all. What we must say is that the representation of three-dimensional space is neither irrelevant nor essential to all art, and that every other sort of representation is irrelevant.

That there is an irrelevant representative or descriptive element in many great works of art is not in the least surprising. Why it is not surprising I shall try to show elsewhere. Representation is not of necessity baneful, and highly realistic forms may be extremely significant. Very often, however, representation is a sign of weakness in an artist. A painter too feeble to create forms that provoke more than a little aesthetic emotion will try to eke that little out by suggesting the emotions of life. To evoke the emotions of life he must use representation. Thus a man will paint an execution, and, fearing to miss with his first barrel of significant form, will try to hit with his second by raising an emotion of fear or pity. But if in the artist an inclination to play upon the emotions of life is often the sign of a flickering inspiration, in the spectator a tendency to seek, behind form, the emotions of life is a sign of defective sensibility always. It means that his aesthetic emotions are weak or, at any rate, imperfect. Before a work of art people who feel little or no emotion for pure form find themselves at a loss. They are deaf men at a concert. They know that they are in the presence of some-thing great, but they lack the power of apprehending it. They know that they ought to feel for it a tremendous emotion, but it happens that the particular kind of emotion it can raise is one that they can feel hardly or not at all. And so they read into the forms of the work those facts and ideas for which they are capable of feeling emotion, and feel for them the emotions that they can feel—the ordinary emotions of life. When confronted by a picture, in-stinctively they refer back its forms to the world from which they came. They treat created form as though it were imitated form, a picture as though it were a photo-graph. Instead of going out on the stream of art into a new world of aesthetic experience, they turn a sharp corner and come straight home to the world of human interests. For them the significance of a work of art depends on what they bring to it; no new thing is added to their lives, only the old material is stirred. A good work of visual art carries a person who is capable of appreciating it out of life into ecstasy: to use art as a means to the emotions of life is to use a telescope for reading the news. You will notice that people who cannot feel pure aesthetic emotions remember pictures by their subjects; whereas people who can, as often as not, have no idea what the subject of a picture is. They have never noticed the representative element, and so when they discuss pictures they talk about the shapes of forms and the relations and quantities of colours. Often they can tell by the quality of a single line whether or no a man is a good artist. They are concerned only with lines and colours, their relations and quantities and qualities; but from these they win an emotion more profound and far more sublime than any that can be given by the description of facts and ideas.

This last sentence has a very confident ring—over-confident, some may think. Perhaps I shall be able to justify it, and make my meaning clearer too, if I give an account of my own feelings about music. I am not really musical. I do not understand music well. I find musical form exceedingly difficult to apprehend, and I am sure that the profounder subtleties of harmony and rhythm more often than not escape me. The form of a musical composition must be simple indeed if I am to grasp it honestly. My opinion about music is not worth having. Yet, sometimes, at a concert, though my appreciation of the music is limited and humble, it is pure. Sometimes, though I have a poor understanding, I have a clean palate. Consequently, when I am feeling bright and clear and intent, at the beginning of a concert for instance, when something that I can grasp is being played, I get from music that pure aesthetic emotion that I get from visual art. It is less intense, and the rapture is evanescent; I understand music too ill for music to transport me far into the world of pure aesthetic ecstasy. But at moments I do appreciate music as pure musical form, as sounds combined according to the laws of a mysterious necessity, as pure art with a tremendous significance of its own and no relation whatever to the significance of life; and in those moments I lose myself in that infinitely sublime state of mind to which pure visual form transports me. How inferior is my normal state of mind at a concert. Tired or perplexed, I let slip my sense of form, my aesthetic emotion collapses, and I begin weaving into the harmonies, that I cannot grasp, the ideas of life. Incapable of feeling the austere emotions of art,

I begin to read into the musical forms human emotions of terror and mystery, love and hate, and spend the minutes, pleasantly enough, in a world of turbid and inferior feeling. At such times, were the grossest pieces of onomatopoeic representation—the song of a bird, the galloping of horses, the cries of children, or the laughing of demons—to be introduced into the symphony, I should not be offended. Very likely I should be pleased; they would afford new points of departure for new trains of romantic feeling or heroic thought. I know very well what has happened. I have been using art as a means to the emotions of life and reading into it the ideas of life. I have been cutting blocks with a razor. I have tumbled from the superb peaks of aesthetic exaltation to the snug foothills of warm humanity. It is a jolly country. No one need be ashamed of enjoying himself there. Only no one who has ever been on the heights can help feeling a little crestfallen in the cosy valleys. And let no one imagine, because he has made merry in the warm tilth and quaint nooks of romance, that he can even guess at the austere and thrilling raptures of those who have climbed the cold, white peaks of art.

About music most people are as willing to be humble as I am. If they cannot grasp musical form and win from it a pure aesthetic emotion, they confess that they understand music imperfectly or not at all. They recognise quite clearly that there is a difference between the feeling of the musician for pure music and that of the cheerful concertgoer for what music suggests. The latter enjoys his own emotions, as he has every right to do, and recognises their inferiority. Unfortunately, people are apt to be less modest about their powers of appreciating visual art. Everyone is inclined to believe that out of pictures, at any rate, he can get all that there is to be got; everyone is ready to cry "humbug" and "impostor" at those who say that more can be had. The good faith of people who feel pure aesthetic emotions is called in question by those who have never felt anything of the sort. It is the prevalence of the representative element, I suppose, that makes the man in the street so sure that he knows a good picture when he sees one. For I have noticed that in matters of architecture, pottery, textiles, &c., ignorance and ineptitude are more willing to defer to the opinions of those who have been blest with peculiar sensibility. It is a pity that cultivated and intelligent men and women cannot be induced to believe that a great gift of aesthetic appreciation is at least as rare in visual as in musical art. A comparison of my own experience in both has enabled me to discriminate very clearly between pure and impure appreciation. Is it too much to ask that others should be as honest about their feelings for pictures as I have been about mine for music? For I am certain that most of those who visit galleries do feel very much what I feel at concerts. They have their moments of pure ecstasy; but the moments are short and unsure. Soon they fall back into the world of human interests and feel emotions, good no doubt, but inferior. I do not dream of saying that what they get from art is bad or nugatory; I say that they do not get the best that art can give. I do not say that they cannot understand art; rather I say that they cannot understand the state of mind of those who understand it best. I do not say that art means nothing or little to them; I say they miss its full significance. I do not suggest for one moment that their appreciation of art is a thing to be ashamed of; the majority of the charming and intelligent people with whom I am acquainted appreciate visual art impurely; and, by the way, the appreciation of almost all great writers has been impure. But provided that there be some fraction of pure aesthetic emotion, even a mixed and minor appreciation of art is, I am sure, one of the most valuable things in the world—so valuable, indeed, that in my giddier moments I have been tempted to believe that art might prove the world's salvation.

Yet, though the echoes and shadows of art enrich the life of the plains, her spirit dwells on the mountains. To him who woos, but woos impurely, she returns enriched what is brought. Like the sun, she warms the good seed in good soil and causes it to bring forth good fruit. But only to the perfect lover does she give a new strange gift

—a gift beyond all price. Imperfect lovers bring to art and take away the ideas and emotions of their own age and civilisation. In twelfth-century Europe a man might have been greatly moved by a Romanesque church and found nothing in a T'ang picture. To a man of a later age, Greek sculpture meant much and Mexican nothing, for only to the former could he bring a crowd of associated ideas to be the objects of familiar emotions. But the perfect lover, he who can feel the profound significance of form, is raised above the accidents of time and place. To him the problems of archaeology, history, and hagiography are impertinent. If the forms of a work are significant its provenance is irrelevant. Before the grandeur of those Sumerian figures in the Louvre he is carried on the same flood of emotion to the same aesthetic ecstasy as, more than four thousand years ago, the Chaldean lover was carried. It is the mark of great art that its appeal is universal and eternal.[1] Significant form stands charged with the power to provoke aesthetic emotion in anyone capable of feeling it. The ideas of men go buzz and die like gnats; men change their institutions and their customs

[1] Mr. Roger Fry permits me to make use of an interesting story that will illustrate my view. When Mr. Okakura, the Government editor of *The Temple Treasures of Japan,* first came to Europe, he found no difficulty in appreciating the pictures of those who from want of will or want of skill did not create illusions but concentrated their energies on the creation of form. He understood immediately the Byzantine masters and the French and Italian Primitives. In the Renaissance painters, on the other hand, with their descriptive preoccupations, their literary and anecdotic interests, he could see nothing but vulgarity and muddle. The universal and essential quality of art, significant form, was missing, or rather had dwindled to a shallow stream, overlaid and hidden beneath weeds, so the universal response, aesthetic emotion, was not evoked. It was not till he came on to Henri-Matisse that he again found himself in the familiar world of pure art. Similarly, sensitive Europeans who respond immediately to the significant forms of great Oriental art, are left cold by the trivial pieces of anecdote and social criticism so lovingly cherished by Chinese dilettanti. It would be easy to multiply instances did not decency forbid the labouring of so obvious a truth.

as they change their coats; the intellectual triumphs of one age are the follies of another; only great art remains stable and unobscure. Great art remains stable and unobscure because the feelings that it awakens are independent of time and place, because its kingdom is not of this world. To those who have and hold a sense of the significance of form what does it matter whether the forms that move them were created in Paris the day before yesterday or in Babylon fifty centuries ago? The forms of art are inexhaustible; but all lead by the same road of aesthetic emotion to the same world of aesthetic ecstasy.

2. AESTHETICS AND POST-IMPRESSIONISM

B Y THE light of my aesthetic hypothesis I can read more clearly than before the history of art; also I can see in that history the place of the contemporary movement. As I shall have a great deal to say about the contemporary movement, perhaps I shall do well to seize this moment, when the aesthetic hypothesis is fresh in my mind and, I hope, in the minds of my readers, for an examination of the movement in relation to the hypothesis. For anyone of my generation to write a book about art that said nothing of the movement dubbed in this country Post-Impressionist would be a piece of pure affectation. I shall have a great deal to say about it, and therefore I wish to see at the earliest possible opportunity how Post-Impressionism stands with regard to my theory of aesthetics. The survey will give me occasion for stating some of the things that Post-Impressionism is and some that it is not. I shall have to raise points that will be dealt with at greater length elsewhere. Here I shall have a chance of raising them, and at least suggesting a solution.

Primitives produce art because they must; they have no other motive than a passionate desire to express their sense of form. Untempted, or incompetent, to create illusions, to the creation of form they devote themselves entirely. Presently, however, the artist is joined by a patron and a public, and soon there grows up a demand for "speaking likenesses." While the gross herd still clamours for likeness, the choicer spirits begin to affect an admiration for cleverness and skill. The end is in sight. In Europe we watch art sinking, by slow degrees, from the thrilling design of Ravenna to the tedious portraiture of Holland, while the grand proportion of Romanesque and Norman architecture becomes Gothic juggling in stone and glass. Before the late noon of the Renaissance art was almost extinct. Only nice illusionists and masters of craft abounded. That was the moment for a Post-Impressionist revival.

For various reasons there was no revolution. The tradition of art remained comatose. Here and there a genius appeared and wrestled with the coils of convention and created significant form. For instance, the art of Nicolas Poussin, Claude, El Greco, Chardin, Ingres, and Renoir, to name a few, moves us as that of Giotto and Cézanne moves. The bulk, however, of those who flourished between the high Renaissance and the contemporary movement may be divided into two classes, virtuosi and dunces. The clever fellows, the minor masters, who might have been artists if painting had not absorbed all their energies, were throughout that period for ever setting themselves technical acrostics and solving them. The dunces continued to elaborate chromophotographs, and continue.

The fact that significant form was the only common quality in the works that moved me, and that in the works that moved me most and seemed most to move the most sensitive people—in primitive art, that is to say—it was almost the only quality, had led me to my hypothesis before ever I became familiar with the works of Cézanne and his followers. Cézanne carried me off my feet before ever I noticed that his strongest characteristic was an insistence on the supremacy of significant form. When I noticed this, my admiration for Cézanne and some of his followers confirmed me in my aesthetic theories. Naturally I had found no difficulty in liking them since I found in them exactly what I liked in everything else that moved me.

There is no mystery about Post-Impressionism; a good Post-Impressionist picture is good for precisely the same reasons that any other picture is good. The essential quality in art is permanent. Post-Impressionism, therefore, implies no violent break with the past. It is merely a deliberate rejection of certain hampering traditions of modern growth.

It does deny that art need ever take orders from the past; but that is not a badge of Post-Impressionism, it is the commonest mark of vitality. Even to speak of Post-Impressionism as a movement may lead to misconceptions; the habit of speaking of movements at all is rather misleading. The stream of art has never run utterly dry: it flows through the ages, now broad now narrow, now deep now shallow, now rapid now sluggish: its colour is changing always. But who can set a mark against the exact point of change? In the earlier nineteenth century the stream ran very low. In the days of the Impressionists, against whom the contemporary movement is in some ways a reaction, it had already become copious. Any attempt to dam and imprison this river, to choose out a particular school or movement and say: "Here art begins and there it ends," is a pernicious absurdity. That way Academization lies. At this moment there are not above half a dozen good painters alive who do not derive, to some extent, from Cézanne, and belong, in some sense, to the Post-Impressionist movement; but tomorrow a great painter may arise who will create significant form by means superficially opposed to those of Cézanne. Superficially, I say, because, essentially, all good art is of the same movement: there are only two kinds of art, good and bad. Nevertheless, the division of the stream into reaches, distinguished by differences of manner, is intelligible and, to historians at any rate, useful. The reaches also differ from each other in volume; one period of art is distinguished from another by its fertility. For a few fortunate years or decades the output of considerable art is great. Suddenly it ceases; or slowly it dwindles: a movement has exhausted itself. How far a movement is made by the fortuitous synchronisation of a number of good artists, and how far the artists are helped to the creation of significant form by the pervasion of some underlying spirit of the age, is a question that can never be decided beyond cavil. But however the credit is to be apportioned—and I suspect it should be divided about equally—we are justified, I think, looking at the history of art as a whole, in regarding such periods of fertility as distinct parts of that whole. Primarily, it is as a period of fertility in good art and artists that I admire the Post-Impressionist movement. Also, I believe that the principles which underlie and inspire that movement are more likely to encourage artists to give of their best, and to foster a good tradition, than any of which modern history bears record. But my interest in this movement, and my admiration for much of the art it has produced, does not blind me to the greatness of the products of other movements; neither, I hope, will it blind me to the greatness of any new creation of form even though that novelty may seem to imply a reaction against the tradition of Cézanne.

Like all sound revolutions, Post-Impressionism is nothing more than a return to first principles. Into a world where the painter was expected to be either a photographer or an acrobat burst the Post-Impressionist, claiming that, above all things, he should be an artist. Never mind, said he, about representation or accomplishment—mind about creating significant form, mind about art. Creating a work of art is so tremendous a business that it leaves no leisure for catching a likeness or displaying address. Every sacrifice made to representation is something stolen from art. Far from being the insolent kind of revolution it is vulgarly supposed to be, Post-Impressionism is, in fact, a return, not indeed to any particular tradition of painting, but to the great tradition of visual art. It sets before every artist the ideal set before themselves by the primitives, an ideal which, since the twelfth century, has been cherished only by exceptional men of genius. Post-Impressionism is nothing but the reassertion of the first commandment of art— Thou shalt create form. By this assertion it shakes hands across the ages with the Byzantine primitives and with every vital movement that has struggled into existence since the arts began.

Post-Impressionism is not a matter of technique. Certainly Cézanne invented a technique, admirably suited to his purpose, which has been adopted and elaborated, more or less, by the majority of his followers. The important thing about a picture, however, is not how it is painted, but whether it provokes aesthetic emotion. As I have said, essentially, a good Post-Impressionist picture resembles all other good works of art, and only differs from some, superficially, by a conscious and deliberate rejection of those technical and sentimental irrelevancies that have been imposed on painting by a bad tradition. This becomes obvious when one visits an exhibition such as the *Salon d' Automne* or *Les Indépendants,* where there are hundreds of pictures in the Post-Impressionist manner, many of which are quite worthless.[1] These, one realises, are bad in precisely the same way as any other picture is bad; their forms are insignificant and compel no aesthetic reaction. In truth, it was an unfortunate necessity that obliged us to speak of "Post-Impressionist pictures," and

[1]Anyone who has visited the very latest French exhibitions will have seen scores of what are called "Cubist" pictures. These afford an excellent illustration of my thesis. Of a hundred cubist pictures three or four will have artistic value. Thirty years ago the same might have been said of "Impressionist" pictures; forty years before that of romantic pictures in the manner of Delacroix. The explanation is simple—the vast majority of those who paint pictures have neither originality nor any considerable talent. Left to themselves they would probably produce the kind of painful absurdity which in England is known as an "Academy picture." But a student who has no original gift may yet be anything but a fool, and many students understand that the ordinary cultivated picture-goer knows an "Academy picture" at a glance and knows that it is bad. Is it fair to condemn severely a young painter for trying to give his picture a factitious interest, or even for trying to conceal beneath striking wrappers the essential mediocrity of his wares? If not heroically sincere he is surely not inhumanly base. Besides, he has to imitate someone, and he likes to be in the fashion. And, after all, a bad cubist picture is no worse than any other bad picture. If anyone is to be blamed, it should be the spectator who cannot distinguish between good cubist pictures and bad. Blame alike the fools who think that because a picture is cubist it must be worthless, and their idiotic enemies who think it must be marvellous. People of sensibility can see that there is as much difference between Picasso and a Montmartre sensationalist as there is between Ingres and the President of the Royal Academy.

now, I think, the moment is at hand when we shall be
able to return to the older and more adequate nomen-
clature, and speak of good pictures and bad. Only we
must not forget that the movement of which Cézanne is
the earliest manifestation, and which has borne so amazing
a crop of good art, owes something, though not everything, to the liberating and revolutionary doctrines of Post-
Impressionism.

The silliest things said about Post-Impressionist pictures
are said by people who regard Post-Impressionism as an
isolated movement, whereas, in fact, it takes its place as
part of one of those huge slopes into which we can divide
the history of art and the spiritual history of mankind. In
my enthusiastic moments I am tempted to hope that it is
the first stage in a new slope to which it will stand in the
same relation as sixth-century Byzantine art stands to the
old. In that case we shall compare Post-Impressionism
with that vital spirit which, towards the end of the fifth
century, flickered into life amidst the ruins of Graeco-
Roman realism. Post-Impressionism, or, let us say the
Contemporary Movement, has a future; but when that
future is present Cézanne and Matisse will no longer be
called Post-Impressionists. They will certainly be called
great artists, just as Giotto and Masaccio are called great
artists; they will be called the masters of a movement; but
whether that movement is destined to be more than a
movement, to be something as vast as the slope that lies
between Cézanne and the masters of S. Vitale, is a matter
of much less certainty than enthusiasts care to suppose.

Post-Impressionism is accused of being a negative and
destructive creed. In art no creed is healthy that is anything
else. You cannot give men genius; you can only give them
freedom—freedom from superstition. Post-Impressionism
can no more make good artists than good laws can make
good men. Doubtless, with its increasing popularity, an
annually increasing horde of nincompoops will employ
the so-called "Post-Impressionist technique" for presenting
insignificant patterns and recounting foolish anecdotes.
Their pictures will be dubbed "Post-Impressionist," but

only by gross injustice will they be excluded from Burlington House. Post-Impressionism is no specific against human folly and incompetence. All it can do for painters is to bring before them the claims of art. To the man of genius and to the student of talent it can say: "Don't waste your time and energy on things that don't matter: concentrate on what does: concentrate on the creation of significant form." Only thus can either give the best that is in him. Formerly because both felt bound to strike a compromise between art and what the public had been taught to expect, the work of one was grievously disfigured, that of the other ruined. Tradition ordered the painter to be photographer, acrobat, archaeologist and littérateur: Post-Impressionism invites him to become an artist.

3. THE METAPHYSICAL
HYPOTHESIS

FOR the present I have said enough about the aesthetic problem and about Post-Impressionism; I want now to consider that metaphysical question—"Why do certain arrangements and combinations of form move us so strangely?" For aesthetics it suffices that they do move us; to all further inquisition of the tedious and stupid it can be replied that, however queer these things may be, they are no queerer than anything else in this incredibly queer universe. But to those for whom my theory seems to open a vista of possibilities I willingly offer, for what they are worth, my fancies.

It seems to me possible, though by no means certain, that created form moves us so profoundly because it expresses the emotion of its creator. Perhaps the lines and colours of a work of art convey to us something that the artist felt. If this be so, it will explain that curious but undeniable fact, to which I have already referred, that what I call material beauty (*e.g.* the wing of a butterfly) does not move most of us in at all the same way as a work of art moves us. It is beautiful form, but it is not significant form. It moves us, but it does not move us aesthetically. It is tempting to explain the difference between "significant form" and "beauty"—that is to say, the difference between form that provokes our aesthetic emotions and form that does not—by saying that significant form conveys to us an emotion felt by its creator and that beauty conveys nothing.

For what, then, does the artist feel the emotion that he is supposed to express? Sometimes it certainly comes to him through material beauty. The contemplation of natural objects is often the immediate cause of the artist's emotion. Are we to suppose, then, that the artist feels, or sometimes feels, for material beauty what we feel for a work of art? Can it be that sometimes for the artist material beauty is somehow significant—that is, capable of provoking aesthetic emotion? And if the form that provokes aesthetic emotion be form that expresses something, can it be that material beauty is to him expressive? Does he feel something behind it as we imagine that we feel something behind the forms of a work of art? Are we to suppose that the emotion which the artist expresses is an aesthetic emotion felt for something the significance of which commonly escapes our coarser sensibilities? All these are questions about which I had sooner speculate than dogmatise.

Let us hear what the artists have got to say for themselves. We readily believe them when they tell us that, in fact, they do not create works of art in order to provoke our aesthetic emotions, but because only thus can they materialise a particular kind of feeling. What, precisely, this feeling is they find it hard to say. One account of the matter, given me by a very good artist, is that what he tries to express in a picture is "a passionate apprehension of form." I have set myself to discover what is meant by "a passionate apprehension of form," and, after much talking and more listening, I have arrived at the following result. Occasionally when an artist—a real artist—looks at objects (the contents of a room, for instance) he perceives them as pure forms in certain relations to each other, and feels emotion for them as such. These are his moments of inspiration: follows the desire to express what has been felt. The emotion that the artist felt in his moment of inspiration he did not feel for objects seen as means, but for objects seen as pure forms—that is, as ends in themselves. He did not feel emotion for a chair as a means to physical well-being, nor as an object associated with the intimate life of a family, nor as the place where someone sat saying things unforgettable, nor yet as a thing bound to the lives of hundreds of men and women, dead or alive, by a hundred subtle ties; doubtless an artist does often feel emotions such as these for the things that he sees, but in the moment of aesthetic vision he sees objects, not as means shrouded in associations, but as pure forms. It is for, or at any rate through, pure form that he feels his inspired emotion.

Now to see objects as pure forms is to see them as ends in themselves. For though, of course, forms are related to each other as parts of a whole, they are related on terms of equality; they are not a means to anything except emotion. But for objects seen as ends in themsleves, do we not feel a profounder and a more thrilling emotion than ever we felt for them as means? All of us, I imagine, do, from time to time, get a vision of material objects as pure forms. We see things as ends in themselves, that is to say; and at such moments it seems possible, and even probable, that we see them with the eye of an artist. Who has not, once at least in his life, had a sudden vision of landscape as pure form? For once, instead of seeing it as fields and cottages, he has felt it as lines and colours. In that moment has he not won from material beauty a thrill indistinguishable from that which art gives? And, if this be so, is it not clear that he has won from material beauty the thrill that, generally, art alone can give, because he has contrived to see it as a pure formal combination of lines and colours? May we go on to say that, having seen it as pure form, having freed it from all casual and adventitious interest, from all that it may have acquired from its commerce with human beings, from all its significance as a means, he has felt its significance as an end in itself?

What is the significance of anything as an end in itself? What is that which is left when we have stripped a thing of all its associations, of all its significance as a means? What is left to provoke our emotion? What but that which philosophers used to call "the thing in itself" and now call "ultimate reality"? Shall I be altogether fantastic in suggesting, what some of the profoundest thinkers have believed, that the significance of the thing in itself is the significance of Reality? Is it possible that the answer to my question, "Why are we so profoundly moved by certain combinations of lines and colours?" should be, "Because artists can express in combinations of lines and colours an emotion felt for reality which reveals itself through line and colour"?

If this suggestion were accepted it would follow that "significant form" was form behind which we catch a sense of ultimate reality. There would be good reason for supposing that the emotions which artists feel in their moments of inspiration, that others feel in the rare moments when they see objects artistically, and that many of us feel when we contemplate works of art, are the same in kind. All would be emotions felt for reality revealing itself through pure form. It is certain that this emotion can be expressed only in pure form. It is certain that most of us can come at it only through pure form. But is pure form the only channel through which anyone can come at this mysterious emotion? That is a disturbing and a most distasteful question, for at this point I thought I saw my way to cancelling out the word "reality," and saying that all are emotions felt for pure form which may or may not have something behind it. To me it would be most satisfactory to say that the reason why some forms move us aesthetically, and others do not, is that some have been so purified that we can feel them aesthetically and that others are so clogged with unaesthetic matter (*e.g.* associations) that only the sensibility of an artist can perceive their pure, formal significance. I should be charmed to believe that it is as certain that everyone must come at reality through form as that everyone must express his sense of it in form. But is that so? What kind of form is that from which the musician draws the emotion that he expresses in abstract harmonies? Whence come the emotions of the architect and the potter? I know that the artist's emotion can be expressed only in form; I know that only by form can my aesthetic emotions be called into play; but can I be sure that it is always by form that an artist's emotion is provoked? Back to reality.

Those who incline to believe that the artist's emotion

is felt for reality will readily admit that visual artists—with whom alone we are concerned—come at reality generally through material form. But don't they come at it sometimes through imagined form? And ought we not to add that sometimes the sense of reality comes we know not whence? The best account I know of this state of being rapt in a mysterious sense of reality is the one that Dante gives:

"O immaginativa, che ne rube
    tal volta sì di fuor, ch' uom non s'accorge
    perchè d'intorno suonin mille tube;

chi move te, se il senso non ti porge?
    Moveti lume, che nel ciel s'informa,
    per sè, o per voler che giù lo scorge.

.   .   .   .   .

e qui fu la mia mente sí ristretta
    dentro da sè, che di fuor non venia
    cosa che fosse allor da lei recetta."

Certainly, in those moments of exaltation that art can give, it is easy to believe that we have been possessed by an emotion that comes from the world of reality. Those who take this view will have to say that there is in all things the stuff out of which art is made—reality; artists, even, can grasp it only when they have reduced things to their purest condition of being—to pure form—unless they be of those who come at it mysteriously unaided by externals; only in pure form can a sense of it be expressed. On this hypothesis the peculiarity of the artist would seem to be that he possesses the power of surely and frequently seizing reality (generally behind pure form), and the power of expressing his sense of it, in pure form always. But many people, though they feel the tremendous significance of form, feel also a cautious dislike for big words; and "reality" is a very big one. These prefer to say that what the artist surprises behind form, or seizes by sheer force of imagination, is the all-pervading rhythm that in-

forms all things; and I have said that I will never quarrel
with that blessed word "rhythm."

The ultimate object of the artist's emotion will remain
for ever uncertain. But, unless we assume that all artists
are liars, I think we must suppose that they do feel an
emotion which they can express in form—and form alone.
And note well this further point; artists try to express emotion, not to make statements about its ultimate or immediate object. Naturally, if an artist's emotion comes to
him from, or through, the perception of forms and formal
relations, he will be apt to express it in forms derived
from those through which it came; but he will not be
bound by his vision. He will be bound by his emotion.
Not what he saw, but only what he felt will necessarily
condition his design. Whether the connection between the
forms of a created work and the forms of the visible
universe be patent or obscure, whether it exist or whether
it does not, is a matter of no consequence whatever. No
one ever doubted that a Sung pot or a Romanesque church
was as much an expression of emotion as any picture that
ever was painted. What was the object of the potter's emotion? What of the builder's? Was it some imagined form,
the synthesis of a hundred different visions of natural
things; or was it some conception of reality, unrelated to
sensual experience, remote altogether from the physical
universe? These are questions beyond all conjecture. In
any case, the form in which he expresses his emotion
bears no memorial of any external form that may have
provoked it. Expression is no wise bound by the forms or
emotions or ideas of life. We cannot know exactly what
the artist feels. We only know what he creates. If reality
be the goal of his emotion, the roads to reality are several.
Some artists come at it through the appearance of things,
some by a recollection of appearance, and some by sheer
force of imagination.

To the question—"Why are we so profoundly moved
by certain combinations of forms?" I am unwilling to
return a positive answer. I am not obliged to, for it is
not an aesthetic question. I do suggest, however, that it

is because they express an emotion that the artist has felt, though I hesitate to make any pronouncement about the nature or object of that emotion. If my suggestion be accepted, criticism will be armed with a new weapon; and the nature of this weapon is worth a moment's consideration. Going behind his emotion and its object, the critic will be able to surprise that which gives form its significance. He will be able to explain why some forms are significant and some are not; and thus he will be able to push all his judgments a step further back. Let me give one example. Of copies of pictures there are two classes; one class contains some works of art, the other none. A literal copy is seldom reckoned even by its owner a work of art. It leaves us cold; its forms are not significant. Yet if it were an absolutely exact copy, clearly it would be as moving as the original, and a photographic reproduction of a drawing often is—almost. Evidently, it is impossible to imitate a work of art exactly; and the differences between the copy and the original, minute though they may be, exist and are felt immediately. So far the critic is on sure and by this time familiar ground. The copy does not move him, because its forms are not identical with those of the original; and just what made the original moving is what does not appear in the copy. But why is it impossible to make an absolutely exact copy? The explanation seems to be that the actual lines and colours and spaces in a work of art are caused by something in the mind of the artist which is not present in the mind of the imitator. The hand not only obeys the mind, it is impotent to make lines and colours in a particular way without the direction of a particular state of mind. The two visible objects, the original and the copy, differ because that which ordered the work of art does not preside at the manufacture of the copy. That which orders the work of art is, I suggest, the emotion which empowers artists to create significant form. The good copy, the copy that moves us, is always the work of one who is possessed by this mysterious emotion. Good copies are never attempts at exact imitation; on examination we find always enormous differences between them and their originals: they are the work of men or women who do not copy but can translate the art of others into their own language. The power of creating significant form depends, not on hawklike vision, but on some curious mental and emotional power. Even to copy a picture one needs, not to see as a trained observer, but to feel as an artist. To make the spectator feel, it seems that the creator must feel too. What is this that imitated forms lack and created forms possess? What is this mysterious thing that dominates the artist in the creation of forms? What is it that lurks behind forms and seems to be conveyed by them to us? What is it that distinguishes the creator from the copyist? What can it be but emotion? Is it not because the artist's forms express a particular kind of emotion that they are significant?—because they fit and envelop it, that they are coherent?—because they communicate it, that they exalt us to ecstasy?

One word of warning is necessary. Let no one imagine that the expression of emotion is the outward and visible sign of a work of art. The characteristic of a work of art is its power of provoking aesthetic emotion; the expression of emotion is possibly what gives it that power. It is useless to go to a picture gallery in search of expression; you must go in search of significant form. When you have been moved by form, you may begin to consider what makes it moving. If my theory be correct, rightness of form is invariably a consequence of rightness of emotion. Right form, I suggest, is ordered and conditioned by a particular kind of emotion; but whether my theory be true or false, the form remains right. If the forms are satisfactory, the state of mind that ordained them must have been aesthetically right. If the forms are wrong, it does not follow that the state of mind was wrong; between the moment of inspiration and the finished work of art there is room for many a slip. Feeble or defective emotion is at best only one explanation of unsatisfactory form. Therefore, when the critic comes across satisfactory form he need not bother about the feelings of the artist; for him to feel the aesthetic significance of the artist's forms suffices. If the artist's state of mind be important, he may be sure that it was right because the forms are right. But when the critic attempts to account for the unsatisfactoriness of forms he may consider the state of mind of the artist. He cannot be sure that because the forms are wrong the state of mind was wrong; because right forms imply right feeling, wrong forms do not necessarily imply wrong feeling; but if he has got to explain the wrongness of form, here is a possibility he cannot overlook. He will have left the firm land of aesthetics to travel in an unstable element; in criticism one catches at any straw. There is no harm in that, provided the critic never forgets that, whatever ingenious theories he may put forward, they can be nothing more than attempts to explain the one central fact—that some forms move us aesthetically and others do not.

This discussion has brought me close to a question that is neither aesthetic nor metaphysical but impinges on both. It is the question of the artistic problem, and it is really a technical question. I have suggested that the task of the artist is either to create significant form or to express a sense of reality—whichever way you prefer to put it. But it is certain that few artists, if any, can sit down or stand up just to create nothing more definite than significant form, just to express nothing more definite than a sense of reality. Artists must canalise their emotion, they must concentrate their energies on some definite problem. The man who sets out with the whole world before him is unlikely to get anywhere. In that fact lies the explanation of the absolute necessity for artistic conventions. That is why it is easier to write good verse than good prose, why it is more difficult to write good blank verse than good rhyming couplets. That is the explanation of the sonnet, the ballade, and the rondeau; severe limitations concentrate and intensify the artist's energies.

It would be almost impossible for an artist who set himself a task no more definite than that of creating, without conditions or limitations material or intellectual, significant form ever so to concentrate his energies as to achieve his object. His objective would lack precision and

therefore his efforts would lack intention. He would almost certainly be vague and listless at his work. It would
seem always possible to pull the thing round by a happy
fluke, it would rarely be absolutely clear that things were
going wrong. The effort would be feeble and the result would
be feeble. That is the danger of aestheticism for the artist.
The man who feels that he has got nothing to do but to
make something beautiful hardly knows where to begin
or where to end, or why he should set about one thing
more than another. The artist has got to feel the necessity
of making his work of art "right." It will be "right" when
it expresses his emotion for reality or is capable of provoking aesthetic emotion in others, whichever way you care
to look at it. But most artists have got to canalise their
emotion and concentrate their energies on some more
definite and more maniable problem than that of making
something that shall be aesthetically "right." They need
a problem that will become the focus of their vast emotions
and vague energies, and when that problem is solved their
work will be "right."

"Right" for the spectator means aesthetically satisfying;
for the artist at work it means the complete realisation of
a conception, the perfect solution of a problem. The mistake that the vulgar make is to suppose that "right" means
the solution of one particular problem. The vulgar are apt
to suppose that the problem which all visual and literary
artists set themselves is to make something lifelike. Now,
all artistic problems—and their possible variety is infinite
—must be the *foci* of one particular kind of emotion, that
specific artistic emotion which I believe to be an emotion
felt for reality, generally perceived through form: but the
nature of the focus is immaterial. It is almost, though not
quite, true to say that one problem is as good as another.
Indeed all problems are, in themselves, equally good,
though, owing to human infirmity, there are two which
tend to turn out badly. One, as we have seen, is the pure
aesthetic problem; the other is the problem of accurate
representation.

The vulgar imagine that there is but one focus, that

"right" means always the realisation of an accurate conception of life. They cannot understand that the immediate problem of the artist may be to express himself within a square or a circle or a cube, to balance certain harmonies, to reconcile certain dissonances, to achieve certain rhythms, or to conquer certain difficulties of medium, just as well as to catch a likeness. This error is at the root of the silly criticism that Mr. Shaw has made it fashionable to print. In the plays of Shakespeare there are details of psychology and portraiture so realistic as to astonish and enchant the multitude, but the conception, the thing that Shakespeare set himself to realise, was not a faithful presentation of life. The creation of Illusion was not the artistic problem that Shakespeare used as a channel for his artistic emotion and a focus for his energies. The world of Shakespeare's plays is by no means so lifelike as the world of Mr. Galsworthy's, and therefore those who imagine that the artistic problem must always be the achieving of a correspondence between printed words or painted forms and the world as they know it are right in judging the plays of Shakespeare inferior to those of Mr. Galsworthy. As a matter of fact, the achievement of verisimilitude, far from being the only possible problem, disputes with the achievement of beauty the honour of being the worst possible. It is so easy to be lifelike, that an attempt to be nothing more will never bring into play the highest emotional and intellectual powers of the artist. Just as the aesthetic problem is too vague, so the representative problem is too simple.

Every artist must choose his own problem. He may take it from wherever he likes, provided he can make it the focus of those artistic emotions he has got to express and the stimulant of those energies he will need to express them. What we have got to remember is that the problem—in a picture it is generally the subject—is of no consequence in itself. It is merely one of the artist's means of expression or creation. In any particular case one problem may be better than another, as a means, just as one canvas or one brand of colours may be; that will depend upon the temperament of the artist, and we may leave it to him.

For us the problem has no value; for the artist it is the working test of absolute "rightness." It is the gauge that measures the pressure of steam; the artist stokes his fires to set the little handle spinning; he knows that his machine will not move until he has got his pointer to the mark; he works up to it and through it; but it does not drive the engine.

What, then, is the conclusion of the whole matter? No more than this, I think. The contemplation of pure form leads to a state of extraordinary exaltation and complete detachment from the concerns of life: of so much, speaking for myself, I am sure. It is tempting to suppose that the emotion which exalts has been transmitted through the forms we contemplate by the artist who created them. If this be so, the transmitted emotion, whatever it may be, must be of such a kind that it can be expressed in any sort of form—in pictures, sculptures, buildings, pots, textiles, &c., &c. Now the emotion that artists express comes to some of them, so they tell us, from the apprehension of the formal significance of material things; and the formal significance of any material thing is the significance of that thing considered as an end in itself. But if an object considered as an end in itself moves us more profoundly (i.e. has greater significance) than the same object considered as a means to practical ends or as a thing related to human interests—and this undoubtedly is the case—we can only suppose that when we consider anything as an end in itself we become aware of that in it which is of greater moment than any qualities it may have acquired from keeping company with human beings. Instead of recognising its accidental and conditioned importance, we become aware of its essential reality, of the God in everything, of the universal in the particular, of the all-pervading rhythm. Call it by what name you will, the thing that I am talking about is that which lies behind the appearance of all things —that which gives to all things their individual significance, the thing in itself, the ultimate reality. And if a more or less unconscious apprehension of this latent reality of material things be, indeed, the cause of that strange emotion, a passion to express which is the inspiration of many artists, it seems reasonable to suppose that those who, unaided by material objects, experience the same emotion have come by another road to the same country.

That is the metaphysical hypothesis. Are we to swallow it whole, accept a part of it, or reject it altogether? Each must decide for himself. I insist only on the rightness of my aesthetic hypothesis. And of one other thing am I sure. Be they artists or lovers of art, mystics or mathematicians, those who achieve ecstasy are those who have freed themselves from the arrogance of humanity. He who would feel the significance of art must make himself humble before it. Those who find the chief importance of art or of philosophy in its relation to conduct or its practical utility—those who cannot value things as ends in themselves or, at any rate, as direct means to emotion—will never get from anything the best that it can give. Whatever the world of aesthetic contemplation may be, it is not the world of human business and passion; in it the chatter and tumult of material existence is unheard, or heard only as the echo of some more ultimate harmony.

II

ART AND LIFE

---

1. ART AND RELIGION

IF IN my first chapter I had been at pains to show that art owed nothing to life the title of my second would invite a charge of inconsistency. The danger would be slight, however; for though art owed nothing to life, life might well owe something to art. The weather is admirably independent of human hopes and fears, yet few of us are so sublimely detached as to be indifferent to the weather. Art does affect the lives of men; it moves to ecstasy, thus giving colour and moment to what might be otherwise a rather grey and trivial affair. Art for some makes life worth living. Also, art is affected by life; for to create art there must be men with hands and a sense of form and colour and three-dimensional space and the power to feel and the passion to create. Therefore art has a great deal to do with life—with emotional life. That it is a means to a state of exaltation is unanimously agreed, and that it comes from the spiritual depths of man's nature is hardly contested. The appreciation of art is certainly a means to ecstasy, and the creation probably the expression of an ecstatic state of mind. Art is, in fact, a necessity to and a product of the spiritual life.

Those who do not part company with me till the last stage of my metaphysical excursion agree that the emotion expressed in a work of art springs from the depths of man's spiritual nature; and those even who will hear nothing of expression agree that the spiritual part is profoundly affected by works of art. Art, therefore, has to do with the spiritual life, to which it gives and from which, I feel sure, it takes. Indirectly, art has something to do with practical life, too; for those emotional experiences must be very faint and contemptible that leave quite untouched our characters. Through its influence on character and point

of view art may affect practical life. But practical life and
human sentiment can affect art only in so far as they can
affect the conditions in which artists work. Thus they may
affect the production of works of art to some extent; to
how great an extent I shall consider in another place.

Also a great many works of visual art are concerned
with life, or rather with the physical universe of which
life is a part, in that the men who created them were
thrown into the creative mood by their surroundings. We
have observed, as we could hardly fail to do, that, whatever the emotion that artists express may be, it comes to
many of them through the contemplation of the familiar
objects of life. The object of an artist's emotion seems to
be more often than not either some particular scene or
object, or a synthesis of his whole visual experience. Art
may be concerned with the physical universe, or with any
part or parts of it, as a means to emotion—a means to
that peculiar spiritual state that we call inspiration. But
the value of these parts as means to anything but emotion
art ignores—that is to say, it ignores their practical utility.
Artists are often concerned with things, but never with
the labels on things. These useful labels were invented
by practical people for practical purposes. The misfortune
is that, having acquired the habit of recognising labels,
practical people tend to lose the power of feeling emotion;
and, as the only way of getting at the thing in itself is by
feeling its emotional significance, they soon begin to lose
their sense of reality. Mr. Roger Fry has pointed out that
few can hope ever to see a charging bull as an end in itself
and yield themselves to the emotional significance of its
forms, because no sooner is the label "Charging Bull"
recognised than we begin to dispose ourselves for flight
rather than contemplation.[1] This is where the habit of
recognising labels serves us well. It serves us ill, however,
when, although there is no call for action or hurry, it comes
between things and our emotional reaction to them. The
label is nothing but a symbol that epitomises for busy

[1] "An Essay in Aesthetics," by Roger Fry: *The New Quar-
terly*, No. 6, vol. ii.

humanity the significance of things regarded as "means."
A practical person goes into a room where there are chairs,
tables, sofas, a hearth-rug and a mantelpiece. Of each
he takes note intellectually, and if he wants to set himself
down or set down a cup, he will know all he needs to
know for his purpose. The label tells him just those facts
that serve his practical ends; of the thing itself that lurks
behind the label nothing is said. Artists, *qua* artists, are
not concerned with labels. They are concerned with things
only as means to a particular kind of emotion, which is
the same as saying that they are only concerned with
things perceived as ends in themselves; for it is only when
things are *perceived* as ends that they *become* means to
this emotion. It is only when we cease to regard the objects
in a landscape as means to anything that we can feel the
landscape artistically. But when we do succeed in regarding
the parts of a landscape as ends in themselves—as pure
forms, that is to say—the landscape becomes *ipso facto*
a means to a peculiar, aesthetic state of mind. Artists are
concerned only with this peculiar emotional significance
of the physical universe: because they *perceive* things as
"ends," things *become* for them "means" to ecstasy.

The habit of recognising the label and overlooking the
thing, of seeing intellectually instead of seeing emotionally,
accounts for the amazing blindness, or rather visual shal-
lowness, of most civilised adults. We do not forget what
has moved us, but what we have merely recognised leaves
no deep impression on the mind. A friend of mine, a man
of taste, desired to make some clearance in his gardens,
encumbered as they were with a multitude of trees; unfortunately most of his friends and all his family objected on
sentimental or aesthetic grounds, declaring that the place
would never be the same to them if the axe were laid to
a single trunk. My friend was in despair, until, one day, I
suggested to him that whenever his people were all away
on visits or travels, as was pretty often the case, he should
have as many trees cut down as could be completely and
cleanly removed during their absence. Since then, several
hundreds have been carted from his small park and pleasure

grounds, and should the secret be betrayed to the family
I am cheerfully confident that not one of them would believe it. I could cite innumerable instances of this insensibility to form. How often have I been one of a party in a
room with which all were familiar, the decoration of which
had lately been changed, and I the only one to notice it.
For practical purposes the room remained unaltered; only
its emotional significance was new. Question your friend
as to the disposition of the furniture in his wife's drawing-
room; ask him to sketch the street down which he passes
daily; ten to one he goes hopelessly astray. Only artists
and educated people of extraordinary sensibility and some
savages and children feel the significance of form so acutely
that they know how things look. These see, because they
see emotionally; and no one forgets the things that have
moved him. Those forget who have never felt the emotional
significance of pure form; they are not stupid nor are they
generally insensitive, but they use their eyes only to collect
information, not to capture emotion. This habit of using
the eyes exclusively to pick up facts is the barrier that
stands between most people and an understanding of visual
art. It is not a barrier that has stood unbreached always,
nor need it stand so for all future time.

In ages of great spiritual exaltation the barrier crumbles
and becomes, in places, less insuperable. Such ages are
commonly called great religious ages; nor is the name ill-
chosen. For, more often than not, religion is the whetstone
on which men sharpen the spiritual sense. Religion, like
art, is concerned with the world of emotional reality, and
with material things only in so far as they are emotionally
significant. For the mystic, as for the artist, the physical
universe is a means to ecstasy. The mystic feels things as
"ends" instead of seeing them as "means." He seeks within
all things that ultimate reality which provokes emotional
exaltation; and, if he does not come at it through pure
form, there are, as I have said, more roads than one to
that country. Religion, as I understand it, is an expression
of the individual's sense of the emotional significance of
the universe; I should not be surprised to find that art

was an expression of the same thing. Anyway, both seem to express emotions different from and transcending the emotions of life. Certainly both have the power of transporting men to superhuman ecstasies; both are means to unearthly states of mind. Art and religion belong to the same world. Both are bodies in which men try to capture and keep alive their shyest and most ethereal conceptions. The kingdom of neither is of this world. Rightly, therefore, do we regard art and religion as twin manifestations of the spirit; wrongly do some speak of art as a manifestation of religion.

If it were said that art and religion were twin manifestations of something that, for convenience sake, may be called "the religious spirit," I should make no serious complaint. But I should insist on the distinction between "religion," in the ordinary acceptation of the word, and "the religious spirit" being stated beyond all possibility of cavil. I should insist that if we are to say that art is a manifestation of the religious spirit, we must say the same of every respectable religion that ever has existed or ever can exist. Above all, I should insist that whoever said it should bear in mind, whenever he said it, that "manifestation" is at least as different from "expression" as Monmouth is from Macedon.

The religious spirit is born of a conviction that some things matter more than others. To those possessed by it there is a sharp distinction between that which is unconditioned and universal and that which is limited and local. It is a consciousness of the unconditioned and universal that makes people religious; and it is this consciousness or, at least, a conviction that some things are unconditioned and universal, that makes their attitude towards the conditioned and local sometimes a little unsympathetic. It is this consciousness that makes them set justice above law, passion above principle, sensibility above culture, intelligence above knowledge, intuition above experience, the ideal above the tolerable. It is this consciousness that makes them the enemies of convention, compromise, and commonsense. In fact, the essence of religion is a conviction that

because some things are of infinite value most are profoundly unimportant, that since the gingerbread is there
one need not feel too strongly about the gilt.

It is useless for liberal divines to pretend that there is no
antagonism between the religious nature and the scientific.
There is no antagonism between religion and science, but
that is a very different matter. In fact, the hypotheses of
science begin only where religion ends: but both religion
and science are born trespassers. The religious and the
scientific both have their prejudices; but their prejudices
are not the same. The scientific mind cannot free itself
from a prejudice against the notion that effects may exist
the causes of which it ignores. Not only do religious minds
manage to believe that there may be effects of which they
do not know, and may never know, the causes—they cannot even see the absolute necessity for supposing that everything is caused. Scientific people tend to trust their senses
and disbelieve their emotions when they contradict them;
religious people tend to trust emotion even though sensual
experience be against it. On the whole, the religious are
the more open-minded. Their assumption that the senses
may mislead is less arrogant than the assumption that
through them alone can we come at reality, for, as Dr.
McTaggart has wittily said, "If a man is shut up in a house,
the transparency of the windows is an essential condition
of his seeing the sky. But it would not be prudent to infer
that, if he walked out of the house, he could not see the
sky, because there was no longer any glass through which
he might see it." [1]

Examples of scientific bigotry are as common as black-
berries. The attitude of the profession towards unorthodox
medicine is the classical instance. In the autumn of 1912
I was walking through the Grafton Galleries with a man
who is certainly one of the ablest, and is reputed one of
the most enlightened, of contemporary men of science.
Looking at the picture of a young girl with a cat by Henri-
Matisse, he exclaimed—"I see how it is, the fellow's astig-
matic." I should have let this bit of persiflage go un-

[1] McTaggart: *Some Dogmas of Religion.*

answered, assuming it to be one of those witty sallies for which the princes of science are so justly famed and to which they often treat us even when they are not in the presence of works of art, had not the professor followed up his clue with the utmost gravity, assuring me at last that no picture in the gallery was beyond the reach of optical diagnostic. Still suspicious of his good faith, I suggested, tentatively, that perhaps the discrepancies between the normal man's vision and the pictures on the wall were the result of intentional distortion on the part of the artists. At this the professor became passionately serious— "Do you mean to tell me," he bawled, "that there has ever been a painter who did not try to make his objects as life-like as possible? Dismiss such silly nonsense from your head." It is the old story: "Clear your mind of cant," that is to say, of anything which appears improbable or un-palatable to Dr. Johnson.

The religious, on the other hand, are apt to be a little prejudiced against common-sense; and, for my own part, I confess that I am often tempted to think that a common-sense view is necessarily a wrong one. It was common-sense to see that the world must be flat and that the sun must go round it; only when those fantastical people made them-selves heard who thought that the solar system could not be quite so simple an affair as common-sense knew it must be were these opinions knocked on the head. Dr. Johnson, the great exemplar of British common-sense, observing in autumn the gathered swallows skimming over pools and rivers, pronounced it certain that these birds sleep all the winter—"A number of them conglobulate together, by flying round and round, and then all in a heap throw them-selves under water, and lie in the bed of a river": how sensibly, too, did he dispose of Berkeley's Idealism— "striking his foot with mighty force against a large stone" —"I refute it thus." Seriously, is the common-sense view ever the right one?

Lately, the men of sense and science have secured allies who have brought to their cause what most it lacked, a little fundamental thought. Those able and honest people,

the Cambridge rationalists, headed by Mr. G. E. Moore, to
whose *Principia Ethica* I owe so much, are, of course, profoundly religious and live by a passionate faith in the
absolute value of certain states of mind; also they have
fallen in love with the conclusions and methods of science.
Being extremely intelligent, they perceive, however, that
empirical arguments can avail nothing for or against a
metaphysical theory, and that ultimately all the conclusions
of science are based on a logic that precedes experience.
Also they perceive that emotions are just as real as sensations. They find themselves confronted, therefore, by this
difficulty; if someone steps forward to say that he has a
direct, disinterested, *a priori*, conviction of the goodness
of his emotions towards the Mass, he puts himself in the
same position as Mr. Moore, who feels a similar conviction
about the goodness of his towards the Truth. If Mr. Moore
is to infer the goodness of one state of mind from his
feelings, why should not someone else infer the goodness
of another from his? The Cambridge rationalists have a
short way with such dissenters. They simply assure them
that they do not feel what they say they feel. Some of them
have begun to apply their cogent methods to aesthetics;
and when we tell them what we feel for pure form they
assure us that, in fact, we feel nothing of the sort. This
argument, however, has always struck me as lacking in
subtlety.

Much as he dislikes mentioning the fact or hearing it
mentioned, the common man of science recognises no other
end in life than protracted and agreeable existence. That is
where he joins issue with the religious; it is also his excuse
for being a eugenist. He declines to believe in any reality
other than that of the physical universe. On that reality he
insists dogmatically.[1] Man, he says, is an animal who, like

[1] I am aware that there are men of science who preserve an
open mind as to the reality of the physical universe, and
recognise that what is known as "the scientific hypothesis"
leaves out of account just those things that seem to us most
real. Doubtless these are the true men of science; they are not
the common ones.

other animals, desires to live; he is provided with senses, and these, like other animals, he seeks to gratify: in these facts he bids us find an explanation of all human aspiration. Man wants to live and he wants to have a good time; to compass these ends he has devised an elaborate machinery. All emotion, says the common man of science, must ultimately be traced to the senses. All moral, religious and aesthetic emotions are derived from physical needs, just as political ideas are based on that gregarious instinct which is simply the result of a desire to live long and to live in comfort. We obey the by-law that forbids us to ride a bicycle on the footpath, because we see that, in the long run, such a law is conducive to continued and agreeable existence, and for very similar reasons, says the man of science, we approve of magnanimous characters and sublime works of art.

"Not so," reply saints, artists, Cambridge rationalists, and all the better sort; for they feel that their religious, aesthetic, or moral emotions are not conditioned, directly or indirectly, by physical needs, nor, indeed, by anything in the physical universe. Some things, they feel, are good, not because they are means to physical well-being, but because they are good in themselves. In nowise does the value of aesthetic or religious rapture depend upon the physical satisfaction it affords. There are things in life the worth of which cannot be related to the physical universe, things of which the worth is not relative but absolute. Of these matters I speak cautiously and without authority: for my immediate purpose—to present my conception of the religious character—I need say only that to some the materialistic conception of the universe does not seem to explain those emotions which they feel with supreme certainty and absolute disinterestedness. The fact is, men of science, having got us into the habit of attempting to justify all our feelings and states of mind by reference to the physical universe, have almost bullied some of us into believing that what cannot be so justified does not exist.

I call him a religious man who, feeling with conviction that some things are good in themselves, and that physical

existence is not amongst them, pursues, at the expense of
physical existence, that which appears to him good. All
those who hold with uncompromising sincerity that spiritual
is more important than material life, are, in my sense, religious. For instance, in Paris I have seen young painters,
penniless, half-fed, unwarmed, ill-clothed, their women and
children in no better case, working all day in feverish
ecstasy at unsaleable pictures, and quite possibly they would
have killed or wounded anyone who suggested a compromise with the market. When materials and credit failed
altogether, they stole newspapers and boot-blacking that
they might continue to serve their masterful passion. They
were superbly religious. All artists are religious. All uncompromising belief is religious. A man who so cares for
truth that he will go to prison, or death, rather than
acknowledge a God in whose existence he does not believe,
is as religious, and as much a martyr in the cause of religion, as Socrates or Jesus. He has set his criterion of values
outside the physical universe.

In material things, half a loaf is said to be better than
no bread. Not so in spiritual. If he thinks that it may do
some good, a politician will support a bill which he considers inadequate. He states his objections and votes with
the majority. He does well, perhaps. In spiritual matters
such compromises are impossible. To please the public the
artist cannot give of his second best. To do so would be to
sacrifice that which makes life valuable. Were he to become
a liar and express something different from what he feels,
truth would no longer be in him. What would it profit him
to gain the whole world and lose his own soul? He knows
that there is that within him which is more important than
physical existence—that to which physical existence is but
a means. That he may feel and express it, it is good that he
should be alive. But unless he may feel and express the best,
he were better dead.

Art and Religion are, then, two roads by which men
escape from circumstance to ecstasy. Between aesthetic and
religious rapture there is a family alliance. Art and Religion
are means to similar states of mind. And if we are licensed

to lay aside the science of aesthetics and, going behind our emotion and its object, consider what is in the mind of the artist, we may say, loosely enough, that art is a manifestation of the religious sense. If it be an expression of emotion—as I am persuaded that it is—it is an expression of that emotion which is the vital force in every religion, or, at any rate, it expresses an emotion felt for that which is the essence of all. We may say that both art and religion are manifestations of man's religious sense, if by "man's religious sense" we mean his sense of ultimate reality. What we may not say is, that art is the expression of any particular religion; for to do so is to confuse the religious spirit with the channels in which it has been made to flow. It is to confuse the wine with the bottle. Art may have much to do with that universal emotion that has found a corrupt and stuttering expression in a thousand different creeds: it has nothing to do with historical facts or metaphysical fancies. To be sure, many descriptive paintings are manifestos and expositions of religious dogmas: a very proper use for descriptive painting too. Certainly the blot on many good pictures is the descriptive element introduced for the sake of edification and instruction. But in so far as a picture is a work of art, it has no more to do with dogmas or doctrines, facts or theories, than with the interests and emotions of daily life.

2. ART AND HISTORY

AND YET there is a connection between art and religion, even in the common and limited sense of that word. There is an historical connection: or, to be more exact, there is a fundamental connection between the history of art and the history of religion. Religions are vital and sincere only so long as they are animated by that which animates all great art—spiritual ferment. It is a mistake, by the way, to suppose that dogmatic religion cannot be vital and sincere. Religious emotions tend always to anchor themselves to earth by a chain of dogma. That tendency is the enemy within the gate of every movement. Dogmatic religion can be vital and sincere, and what is more, theology and ritual have before now been the trumpet and drum of spiritual revolutions. But dogmatic or intellectually free, religious ages, ages of spiritual turmoil, ages in which men set the spirit above the flesh and the emotions above the intellect, are the ages in which is felt the emotional significance of the universe. Then it is men live on the frontiers of reality and listen eagerly to travellers' tales. Thus it comes about that the great ages of religion are commonly the great ages of art. As the sense of reality grows dim, as men become more handy at manipulating labels and symbols, more mechanical, more disciplined, more specialised, less capable of feeling things directly, the power of escaping to the world of ecstasy decays, and art and religion begin to sink. When the majority lack, not only the emotion out of which art and religion are made, but even the sensibility to respond to what the few can still offer, art and religion founder. After that, nothing is left of art and religion but their names;

71

illusion and prettiness are called art, politics and sentimentality religion.

Now, if I am right in thinking that art is a manifestation
—a manifestation, mark, and not an expression—of man's
spiritual state, then in the history of art we shall read the
spiritual history of the race. I am not surprised that those
who have devoted their lives to the study of history should
take it ill when one who professes only to understand the
nature of art hints that by understanding his own business
he may become a judge of theirs. Let me be as conciliatory
as possible. No one can have less right than I, or, indeed,
less inclination to assume the proud title of "scientific
historian": no one can care less about historical small-talk
or be more at a loss to understand what precisely is meant
by "historical science." Yet if history be anything more than
a chronological catalogue of facts, if it be concerned with
the movements of mind and spirit, then I submit that to
read history aright we must know, not only the works of art
that each age produced, but also their value as works of
art. If the aesthetic significance or insignificance of works
of art does, indeed, bear witness to a spiritual state, then
he who can appreciate that significance should be in a
position to form some opinion concerning the spiritual state
of the men who produced those works and of those who
appreciated them. If art be at all the sort of thing it is
commonly supposed to be, the history of art must be an
index to the spiritual history of the race. Only, the historian
who wishes to use art as an index must possess not merely
the nice observation of the scholar and the archaeologist,
but also a fine sensibility. For it is the aesthetic significance
of a work that gives a clue to the state of mind that produced it; so the ability to assign a particular work to a
particular period avails nothing unaccompanied by the
power of appreciating its aesthetic significance.

To understand completely the history of an age must we
know and understand the history of its art? It seems so.
And yet the idea is intolerable to scientific historians. What
becomes of the great scientific principle of water-tight com-

partments? Again, it is unjust: for assuredly, to understand art we need know nothing whatever about history. It may be that from works of art we can draw inferences as to the sort of people who made them: but the longest and most intimate conversations with an artist will not tell us whether his pictures are good or bad. We must see them: then we shall know. I may be partial or dishonest about the work of my friend, but its aesthetic significance is not more obvious to me than that of a work that was finished five thousand years ago. To appreciate fully a work of art we require nothing but sensibility. To those that can hear Art speaks for itself: facts and dates do not; to make bricks of such stuff one must glean the uplands and hollows for tags of auxiliary information and suggestion; and the history of art is no exception to the rule. To appreciate a man's art I need know nothing whatever about the artist; I can say whether this picture is better than that without the help of history; but if I am trying to account for the deterioration of his art, I shall be helped by knowing that he has been seriously ill or that he has married a wife who insists on his boiling her pot. To mark the deterioration was to make a pure, aesthetic judgment: to account for it was to become an historian. To understand the history of art we must know something of other kinds of history. Perhaps, to understand thoroughly any kind of history we must understand every kind of history. Perhaps the history of an age or of a life is an indivisible whole. Another intolerable idea! What becomes of the specialist? What of those formidable compendiums in which the multitudinous activities of man are kept so jealously apart? The mind boggles at the monstrous vision of its own conclusions.

But, after all, does it matter to me? I am not an historian of art or of anything else. I care very little when things were made, or why they were made; I care about their emotional significance to us. To the historian everything is a means to some other means; to me everything that matters is a direct means to emotion. I am writing about art, not about history. With history I am concerned only in so far as history serves to illustrate my hypothesis: and whether history be true or false matters very little, since my hypothesis is not based on history but on personal experience, not on facts but on feelings. Historical fact and falsehood are of no consequence to people who try to deal with realities. They need not ask, "Did this happen?"; they need ask only, "Do I feel this?" Lucky for us that it is so: for if our judgments about real things had to wait upon historical certitude they might have to wait for ever. Nevertheless it is amusing to see how far that of which we are sure agrees with that which we should expect. My aesthetic hypothesis—that the essential quality in a work of art is significant form—was based on my aesthetic experience. Of my aesthetic experiences I am sure. About my second hypothesis, that significant form is the expression of a peculiar emotion felt for reality—I am far from confident. However, I assume it to be true, and go on to suggest that this sense of reality leads men to attach greater importance to the spiritual than to the material significance of the universe, that it disposes men to feel things as ends instead of merely recognising them as means, that a sense of reality is, in fact, the essence of spiritual health. If this be so, we shall expect to find that ages in which the creation of significant form is checked are ages in which the sense of reality is dim, and that these ages are ages of spiritual poverty. We shall expect to find the curves of art and spiritual fervour ascending and descending together. In my next chapter I shall glance at the history of a cycle of art with the intention of following the movement of art and discovering how far that movement keeps pace with changes in the spiritual state of society. My view of the rise, decline and fall of art in Christendom is based entirely on a series of independent aesthetic judgments in the rightness of which I have the arrogance to feel considerable confidence. I pretend to a power of distinguishing between significant and insignificant form, and it will interest me to see whether a decline in the significance of forms—a deterioration of art, that is to say—synchronises generally with a lowering of the religious sense. I shall expect to find that whenever artists have allowed themselves to be seduced from their proper business, the creation of form, by other and irrelevant interests, society has been spiritually decadent. Ages in which the sense of formal significance has been swamped utterly by preoccupation with the obvious, will turn out, I suspect, to have been ages of spiritual famine. Therefore, while following the fortunes of art across a period of fourteen hundred years, I shall try to keep an eye on that of which art may be a manifestation—man's sense of ultimate reality.

To criticise a work of art historically is to play the science-besotted fool. No more disastrous theory ever issued from the brain of a charlatan than that of evolution in art. Giotto did not creep, a grub, that Titian might flaunt, a butterfly. To think of a man's art as leading on to the art of someone else is to misunderstand it. To praise or abuse or be interested in a work of art because it leads or does not lead to another work of art is to treat it as though it were not a work of art. The connection of one work of art with another may have everything to do with history: it has nothing to do with appreciation. So soon as we begin to consider a work as anything else than an end in itself we leave the world of art. Though the development of painting from Giotto to Titian may be interesting histori-cally, it cannot affect the value of any particular picture: aesthetically, it is of no consequence whatever. Every work of art must be judged on its own merits.

Therefore, be sure that, in my next chapter, I am not going to make aesthetic judgments in the light of history; I am going to read history in the light of aesthetic judgments. Having made my judgments, independently of any theory, aesthetic or non-aesthetic, I shall be amused to see how far the view of history that may be based on them agrees with accepted historical hypotheses. If my judgments and the dates furnished by historians be correct, it will follow that some ages have produced more good art than others: but, indeed, it is not disputed that the variety in the artistic significance of different ages is immense. I shall be curious to see what relation can be established between the art and the age that produced it. If my second hypothesis—that

art is the expression of an emotion for ultimate reality—
be correct, the relation between art and its age will be
inevitable and intimate. In that case, an aesthetic judgment
will imply some sort of judgment about the general state of
mind of the artist and his admirers. In fact, anyone who
accepts absolutely my second hypothesis with all its possible
implications—which is more than I am willing to do—will
not only see in the history of art the spiritual history of
the race, but will be quite unable to think of one without
thinking of the other.

If I do not go quite so far as that, I stop short only by a
little. Certainly it is less absurd to see in art the key to
history than to imagine that history can help us to an
appreciation of art. In ages of spiritual fervour I look for
great art. By ages of spiritual fervour I do not mean
pleasant or romantic or humane or enlightened ages; I
mean ages in which, for one reason or another, men have
been unusually excited about their souls and unusually
indifferent about their bodies. Such ages, as often as not,
have been superstitious and cruel. Preoccupation with the
soul may lead to superstition, indifference about the body to
cruelty. I never said that ages of great art were sympathetic
to the middle-classes. Art and a quiet life are incompatible
I think; some stress and turmoil there must be. Need I add
that in the snuggest age of materialism great artists may
arise and flourish? Of course: but when the production of
good art is at all widespread and continuous, near at hand
I shall expect to find a restless generation. Also, having
marked a period of spiritual stir, I shall look, not far off,
for its manifestation in significant form. But the stir must be
spiritual and genuine; a swirl of emotionalism or political
frenzy will provoke nothing fine.[1] How far in any particular
age the production of art is stimulated by general exaltation,

[1] I should not have expected the wars of so-called religion
or the Puritan revolution to have awakened in men a sense
of the emotional significance of the universe, and I should
be a good deal surprised if Sir Edward Carson's agitation were
to produce in the North-East of Ireland a crop of first-rate
formal expression.

or general exaltation by works of art, is a question hardly to be decided. Wisest, perhaps, is he who says that the two seem to have been interdependent. Just how dependent I believe them to have been, will appear when, in my next chapter, I attempt to sketch the rise, decline, and fall of the Christian slope.

3. ART AND ETHICS

BETWEEN me and the pleasant places of history remains, however, one ugly barrier. I cannot dabble and paddle in the pools and shallows of the past until I have answered a question so absurd that the nicest people never tire of asking it: "What is the moral justification of art?" Of course they are right who insist that the creation of art must be justified on ethical grounds: all human activities must be so justified. It is the philosopher's privilege to call upon the artist to show that what he is about is either good in itself or a means to good. It is the artist's duty to reply: "Art is good because it exalts to a state of ecstasy better far than anything a benumbed moralist can even guess at; so shut up." Philosophically he is quite right; only, philosophy is not so simple as that. Let us try to answer philosophically.

The moralist inquires whether art is either good in itself or a means to good. Before answering, we will ask what he means by the word "good," not because it is in the least doubtful, but to make him think. In fact, Mr. G. E. Moore has shown pretty conclusively in his *Principia Ethica* that by "good" everyone means just good. We all know quite well what we mean though we cannot define it. "Good" can no more be defined than "Red": no quality can be defined. Nevertheless we know perfectly well what we mean when we say that a thing is "good" or "red." This is so obviously true that its statement has greatly disconcerted, not to say enraged, the orthodox philosophers.

Orthodox philosophers are by no means agreed as to what we do mean by "good," only they are sure that we cannot mean what we say. They used to be fond of assuming that "good" meant pleasure; or, at any rate, that pleasure was the sole good as an end: two very different propositions. That "good" means "pleasure" and that

79

pleasure is the sole good was the opinion of the Hedonists, and is still the opinion of any Utilitarians who may have lingered on into the twentieth century. They enjoy the honour of being the only ethical fallacies worth the powder and shot of a writer on art. I can imagine no more delicate or convincing piece of logic than that by which Mr. G. E. Moore disposes of both. But it is none of my business to do clumsily what Mr. Moore has done exquisitely. I have no mind by attempting to reproduce his dialectic to incur the merited ridicule of those familiar with the *Principia Ethica* or to spoil the pleasure of those who will be wise enough to run out this very minute and order a master-piece with which they happen to be unacquainted. For my immediate purpose it is necessary only to borrow one shaft from that well-stocked armoury.

To him who believes that pleasure is the sole good, I will put this question: Does he, like John Stuart Mill, and everyone else I ever heard of, speak of "higher and lower" or "better and worse" or "superior and inferior" pleasures? And, if so, does he not perceive that he has given away his case? For, when he says that one pleasure is "higher" or "better" than another, he does not mean that it is greater in *quantity* but superior in *quality*.

On page 7 of *Utilitarianism,* J. S. Mill says:—

"If one of the two (pleasures) is, by those who are competently acquainted with both, placed so far above the other that they prefer it, even though knowing it to be attended with a greater amount of discontent, and would not resign it for any quantity of the other pleasure which their nature is capable of, we are justified in ascribing to the preferred enjoyment a superiority in quality, so far out-weighing quantity as to render it, in comparison, of small account."

But if pleasure be the sole good, the only possible criterion of pleasures is quantity of pleasure. "Higher" or "better" can only mean containing more pleasure. To speak of "better pleasures" in any other sense is to make the goodness of the sole good as an end depend upon something which, *ex hypothesi,* is not good as an end. Mill is as one who, having set up sweetness as the sole good quality in jam, prefers Tiptree to Crosse and Blackwell, not because it is sweeter, but because it possesses a better kind of sweetness. To do so is to discard sweetness as an ultimate criterion and to set up something else in its place. So, when Mill, like everyone else, speaks of "better" or "higher" or "superior" pleasures, he discards pleasure as an ultimate criterion, and thereby admits that pleasure is not the sole good. He feels that some pleasures are better than others, and determines their respective values by the degree in which they possess that quality which all recognise but none can define—goodness. By higher and lower, superior and inferior pleasures we mean simply more good and less good pleasures. There are, therefore, two different qualities, Pleasantness and Goodness. Pleasure, amongst other things, may be good; but pleasure cannot mean good. By "good" we cannot mean "pleasureable"; for, as we see, there is a quality, "goodness," so distinct from pleasure that we speak of pleasures that are more or less good without meaning pleasures that are more or less pleasant. By "good," then, we do not mean "pleasure," neither is pleasure the sole good.

Mr. Moore goes on to inquire what things are good in themselves, as ends that is to say. He comes to a conclusion with which we all agree, but for which few could have found convincing and logical arguments: "states of mind," he shows, alone are good as ends.[1] People who have very little taste for logic will find a simple and satisfactory proof of this conclusion afforded by what is called "the method of isolation."

That which is good as an end will retain some, at any rate, of its value in complete isolation: it will retain all its value as an end. That which is good as a means only will lose all its value in isolation. That which is good as an end will remain valuable even when deprived of all its consequences and left with nothing but bare existence. There-

[1] Formerly he held that inanimate beauty also was good in itself. But this tenet, I am glad to learn, he has discarded.

fore, we can discover whether honestly we feel something to be good as an end, if only we can conceive it in complete isolation, and be sure that so isolated it remains valuable. Bread is good. Is bread good as an end or as a means? Conceive a loaf existing in an uninhabited and uninhabitable planet. Does it seem to lose its value? That is a little too easy. The physical universe appears to most people immensely good, for towards nature they feel violently that emotional reaction which brings to the lips the epithet "good"; but if the physical universe were not related to mind, if it were never to provoke an emotional reaction, if no mind were ever to be affected by it, and if it had no mind of its own, would it still appear good? There are two stars: one is, and ever will be, void of life, on the other exists a fragment of just living protoplasm which will never develop, will never become conscious. Can we say honestly that we feel one to be better than the other? Is life itself good as an end? A clear judgment is made difficult by the fact that one cannot conceive anything without feeling something for it; one's very conceptions provoke states of mind and thus acquire value as means. Let us ask ourselves, bluntly, can that which has no mind and affects no mind have value? Surely not. But anything which has a mind can have intrinsic value, and anything that affects a mind may become valuable as a means, since the state of mind produced may be valuable in itself. Isolate that mind. Isolate the state of mind of a man in love or rapt in contemplation; it does not seem to lose all its value. I do not say that its value is not decreased; obviously, it loses its value as a means to producing good states of mind in others. But a certain value does subsist—an intrinsic value. Populate the lone star with one human mind and every part of that star becomes potentially valuable as a means, because it may be a means to that which is good as an end —a good state of mind. The state of mind of a person in love or rapt in contemplation suffices in itself. We do not stay to inquire "What useful purpose does this serve, whom does it benefit, and how?" We say directly and with conviction—"This is good."

When we are challenged to justify our opinion that anything, other than a state of mind, is good, we, feeling it to be a means only, do very properly seek its good effects, and our last justification is always that it produces good states of mind. Thus, when asked why we call a patent fertiliser good, we may, if we can find a listener, show that the fertiliser is a means to good crops, good crops a means to food, food a means to life, and life a necessary condition of good states of mind. Further we cannot go. When asked why we hold a particular state of mind to be good, the state of aesthetic contemplation for instance, we can but reply that to us its goodness is self-evident. Some states of mind appear to be good independently of their consequences. No other things appear to be good in this way. We conclude, therefore, that good states of mind are alone good as ends.

To justify ethically any human activity, we must inquire—"Is this a means to good states of mind?" In the case of art our answer will be prompt and emphatic. Art is not only a means to good states of mind, but, perhaps, the most direct and potent that we possess. Nothing is more direct, because nothing affects the mind more immediately; nothing is more potent, because there is no state of mind more excellent or more intense than the state of aesthetic contemplation. This being so, to seek any other moral justification for art, to seek in art a means to anything less than good states of mind, is an act of wrongheadedness to be committed only by a fool or a man of genius.

Many fools have committed it and one man of genius has made it notorious. Never was cart put more obstructively before horse than when Tolstoi announced that the justification of art was its power of promoting good actions. As if actions were ends in themselves! There is neither virtue nor vice in running: but to run with good tidings is commendable, to run away with an old lady's purse is not. There is no merit in shouting: but to speak up for truth and justice is well, to deafen the world with charlatanry is damnable. Always it is the end in view that gives value to

action; and, ultimately, the end of all good actions must
be to create or encourage or make possible good states of
mind. Therefore, inciting people to good actions by means
of edifying images is a respectable trade and a roundabout
means to good. Creating works of art is as direct a means
to good as a human being can practise. Just in this fact lies
the tremendous importance of art: there is no more direct
means to good.

To pronounce anything a work of art is, therefore, to
make a momentous moral judgment. It is to credit an
object with being so direct and powerful a means to good
that we need not trouble ourselves about any other of its
possible consequences. But even were this not the case,
the habit of introducing moral considerations into judgments between particular works of art would be inexcusable.
Let the moralist make a judgment about art as a whole, let
him assign it what he considers its proper place amongst
means to good, but in aesthetic judgments, in judgments
between members of the same class, in judgments between
works of art considered as art, let him hold his tongue. If
he esteem art anything less than equal to the greatest means
to good he mistakes. But granting, for the sake of peace, its
inferiority to some, I will yet remind him that his moral
judgments about the value of particular works of art have
nothing to do with their artistic value. The judge at Epsom
is not permitted to disqualify the winner of the Derby in
favour of the horse that finished last but one on the ground
that the latter is just the animal for the Archbishop of
Canterbury's brougham.

Define art as you please, preferably in accordance with
my ideas; assign it what place you will in the moral system;
and then discriminate between works of art according to
their excellence in that quality, or those qualities, that you
have laid down in your definition as essential and peculiar
to works of art. You may, of course, make ethical judgments about particular works, not as works of art, but as
members of some other class, or as independent and un-
classified parts of the universe. You may hold that a particular picture by the President of the Royal Academy is a

greater means to good than one by the glory of the New English Art Club, and that a penny bun is better than either. In such a case you will be making a moral and not an aesthetic judgment. Therefore it will be right to take into account the area of the canvases, the thickness of the frames, and the potential value of each as fuel or shelter against the rigours of our climate. In casting up accounts you should not neglect their possible effects on the middle-aged people who visit Burlington House and the Suffolk Street Gallery; nor must you forget the consciences of those who handle the Chantry funds, or of those whom high prices provoke to emulation. You will be making a moral and not an aesthetic judgment; and if you have concluded that neither picture is a work of art, though you may be wasting your time, you will not be making yourself ridiculous. But when you treat a picture as a work of art, you have, unconsciously perhaps, made a far more important moral judgment. You have assigned it to a class of objects so powerful and direct as means to spiritual exaltation that all minor merits are inconsiderable. Paradoxical as it may seem, the only relevant qualities in a work of art, judged as art, are artistic qualities: judged as a means to good, no other qualities are worth considering; for there are no qualities of greater moral value than artistic qualities, since there is no greater means to good than art.

III

THE CHRISTIAN SLOPE

1. THE RISE OF CHRISTIAN ART

WHAT do I mean by a slope? That I hope to make
clear in the course of this chapter and the next. But,
as readers may expect something to go on with, I will
explain immediately that, though I recognise the continuity
of the stream of art, I believe that it is possible and proper
to divide that stream into slopes and movements. About
the exact line of division there can be no certainty. It is
easy to say that in the passage of a great river from the
hills to the sea, the depth, the width, the colour, the
temperature, and the velocity of the waters are bound to
change; to fix precisely the point of change is another
matter. If I try to picture for myself the whole history of
art from earliest times in all parts of the world I am
unable, of course, to see it as a single thread. The stuff of
which it is made is unchangeable, it is always water that
flows down the river, but there is more than one channel:
for instance, there is European art and Oriental. To me
the universal history of art has the look of a map in which
several streams descend from the same range of mountains
to the same sea. They start from different altitudes but all
descend at last to one level. Thus, I should say that the
slope at the head of which stand the Buddhist masterpieces
of the Wei, Liang, and T'ang dynasties begins a great deal
higher than the slope at the head of which are the Greek
primitives of the seventh century, and higher than that of
which early Sumerian sculpture is the head; but when we
have to consider contemporary Japanese art, Graeco-
Roman and Roman sculpture, and late Assyrian, we see
that all have found the same sea-level of nasty naturalism.

By a slope, then, I mean that which lies between a great
primitive morning, when men create art because they must,
and that darkest hour when men confound imitation with

~~art~~. These slopes can be subdivided into movements. The downward course of a slope is not smooth and even, but broken and full of accidents. Indeed the procession of art does not so much resemble a river as a road from the mountains to the plain. ~~That road is a sequence of ups and downs.~~ An up and a down together form a movement. Sometimes the apex of one movement seems to reach as high as the apex of the movement that preceded it, but always its base carries us farther down the slope. Also, in the history of art the summit of one movement seems always to spring erect from the trough of its predecessor. The upward stroke is vertical, the downward an inclined plane. For instance, from Duccio to Giotto is a step up, sharp and shallow. From Giotto to Lionardo is a long and, at times, almost imperceptible fall. Duccio is a fine decadent of that Basilian movement which half survived the Latin conquest and came to an exquisite end under the earlier Palaeologi. The peak of that movement rises high above Giotto, though Duccio near its base is below him. Giotto's art is definitely inferior to the very finest Byzantine of the eleventh and twelfth centuries, and Giotto is the crest of a new movement destined and doomed inevitably to sink to depths undreamed of by Duccio.

All that was spiritual in Greek civilisation was sick before the sack of Corinth, and all that was alive in Greek art had died many years earlier. That it had died before the death of Alexander let his tomb at Constantinople be my witness. Before they set the last stone of the Parthenon it was ailing: the big marbles in the British Museum are the last significant examples of Greek art; the frieze, of course, proves nothing, being mere artisan work. But the man who made what one may as well call "The Theseus" and "The Ilissus," the man whom one may as well call Phidias, crowns the last vital movement in the Hellenic slope. He is a genius, but he is no oddity: he falls quite naturally into his place as the master of the early decadence; he is the man in whom runs rich and fast but a little coarsened the stream of inspiration that gave life to archaic Greek sculpture. He is the Giotto—but an inferior Giotto—of the slope

Oct. 26, 1973

that starts from the eighth century B.C.—so inferior to the sixth century A.D.—to peter out in the bogs of Hellenistic and Roman rubbish. Whence sprang that ~~Hellenic impulse?~~ As yet we cannot tell. ~~Probably, from the ruins of some venerable Mediterranean civility, against the complex materialism of which it was, in its beginnings, I dare say, a reaction.~~ The story of its prime can be read in fragments of archaic sculpture scattered throughout Europe, and studied in the National Museum at Athens, where certain statues of athletes, dating from about 600, reveal the excellences and defects of Greek art at its best. Of its early decline in the fifth century Phidias is the second-rate Giotto; the copies of his famous contemporaries and immediate predecessors are too loathsome to be at all just; Praxiteles, in the fourth century, the age of accomplished prettiness, is the Correggio, or whatever delightful trifler your feeling for art and chronology may suggest. Fifth and fourth century architecture forbid us to forget the greatness of the Greeks in the golden age of their intellectual and political history. The descent from sensitive, though always rather finikin, drawing through the tasteful and accomplished to the feebly forcible may be followed in the pots and vases of the sixth, fifth, fourth, and third centuries. In the long sands and flats of Roman realism the stream of Greek inspiration is lost for ever.

Before the death of Marcus Aurelius, Europe was as weary of materialism as England before the death of Victoria. But what power was to destroy a machine that had enslaved men so completely that they dared not conceive an alternative? The machine was grown so huge that man could no longer peer over its side; man could see nothing but its cranks and levers, could hear nothing but its humming, could mark the spinning fly-wheel and fancy himself in contemplation of the revolving spheres. Annihilation was the only escape for the Roman citizen from the Roman Empire. Yet, while in the West Hadrian was raising the Imperial talent for brutalisation to a system and a science, somewhere in the East, in Egypt, or in Asia Minor, or, more probably in Syria, in Mesopotamia, or

even Persia, the new leaven was at work. That power
which was to free the world was in ferment. The religious
spirit was again coming to birth. Here and there, in face
of the flat contradiction of circumstances, one would arise
and assert that man does not live by bread alone. Orphism,
Mythraism, Christianity, many forms of one spirit, were
beginning to mean something more than curious ritual
and discreet debauch. Very slowly a change was coming
over the face of Europe.

There was change before the signs of it became apparent.
The earliest Christian paintings in the catacombs are purely
classical. If the early Christians felt anything new they
could not express it. But before the second century was
out Coptic craftsmen had begun to weave into dead Roman
designs something vital. The academic patterns are queerly
distorted and flattened out into forms of a certain significance, as we can feel for ourselves if we go to the
textile room at South Kensington. Certainly, these second
century Coptic textiles are more like works of art than
anything that had been produced in the Roman Empire
for more than four hundred years. Egyptian paintings of
the third century bear less positive witness to the fumblings
of a new spirit. But at the beginning of the fourth century
Diocletian built his palace at Spalato, where we have all
learned to see classicism and the new spirit from the East
fighting it out side by side; and, if we may trust Strzygow-
ski, from the end of that century dates the beautiful church
of Kodja-Kalessi in Isauria. The century in which the East
finally dominated the West (350-450) is a period of incubation. It is a time of disconcerting activity that precedes
the unmistakable launch of art upon the Christian slope.
I would confidently assert that every artistic birth is preceded by a period of uneasy gestation in which the unborn
child acquires the organs and energy that are to carry it
forward on its long journey, if only I possessed the data
that would give a tottering support to so comforting a
generalisation. Alas! the births of the great slopes of antiquity are shrouded in a night scarcely ruffled by the
minute researches of patient archaeologists and impervious

to the startling discoveries by experts of more or less palpable forgeries. Of these critical periods we dare not speak confidently; nevertheless we can compare the fifth century with the nineteenth and draw our own conclusions.

In 450 they built the lovely Galla Placidia at Ravenna. It is a building essentially un-Roman; that is to say, the Romanism that clings to it is accidental and adds nothing to its significance. The mosaics within, however, are still coarsely classical. There is a nasty, woolly realism about the sheep, and about the good shepherd more than a suspicion of the stodgy, Graeco-Roman, Apollo. Imitation still fights, though it fights a losing battle, with significant form. When S. Vitale was begun in 526 the battle was won. Sta. Sophia at Constantinople was building between 532 and 537; the finest mosaics in S. Vitale, S. Apollinare-Nuovo and S. Apollinare-in-Classe belong to the sixth century; so do SS. Sergius and Bacchus at Constantinople and the Duomo at Parenzo. In fact, to the sixth century belong the most majestic monuments of Byzantine art. It is the primitive and supreme summit of the Christian slope. The upward spring from the levels of Graeco-Romanism is immeasurable. The terms in which it could be stated have yet to be discovered. It is the whole length of the slope from Sta. Sophia to the Victoria Memorial pushed upright to stand on a base of a hundred years. We are on heights from which the mud-flats are invisible; resting here, one can hardly believe that the flats ever were, or, at any rate, that they will ever be again. Go to Ravenna, and you will see the masterpieces of Christian art, the primitives of the slope: go to the Tate Gallery or the Luxembourg, and you will see the end of that slope—Christian art at its last gasp. These *memento mori* are salutary in an age of assurance when, looking at the pictures of Cézanne, we feel, not inexcusably, that we are high above the mud and malaria. Between Cézanne and another Tate Gallery, what lies in store for the human spirit? Are we in the period of a new incubation? Or is the new age born? Is it a new slope that we are on, or are we merely part of a surprisingly vigorous premonitory flutter? These are queries to ponder. Is Cézanne the beginning of a slope, a portent, or merely the crest of a movement? The oracles are dumb. This alone seems to me sure: ~~since the Byzantine primitives set their mosaics at Ravenna no artist in Europe has created forms of greater significance unless it be Cézanne.~~

With Sta. Sophia at Constantinople, and the sixth century churches and mosaics at Ravenna, the Christian slope establishes itself in Europe.[1] In the same century it took a downward twist at Constantinople; but in one part of Europe or another the new inspiration continued to manifest itself supremely for more than six hundred years. There were ups and downs, of course, movements and reactions; in some places art was almost always good, in others it was never first-rate; but there was no universal, irreparable depreciation till Norman and Romanesque architecture gave way to Gothic, till twelfth-century sculpture became thirteenth-century figuration.

~~Christian art preserved its primitive significance for more than half a millennium.~~ Therein I see no marvel. Even ideas and emotions travelled slowly in those days. In one respect, at any rate, trains and steamboats have fulfilled the predictions of their exploiters—they have made everything move faster: the mistake lies in being quite so positive that this is a blessing. In those dark ages things moved slowly; that is one reason why the new force had not spent itself in six hundred years. Another is that the revelation came to an age that was constantly breaking fresh ground. Always there was a virgin tract at hand to take the seed and raise a lusty crop. Between 500 and 1000 A.D. the population of Europe was fluid. Some new race was always catching the inspiration and feeling and

[1] I am not being so stupid as to suggest that in the sixth century the Hellenistic influence died. It persisted for another 300 years at least. In sculpture and ivory carving it was only ousted by the Romanesque movement of the eleventh century. Inevitably a great deal of Hellenistic stuff continued to be produced after the rise of Byzantine art. For how many years after the maturity of Cézanne will painters continue to produce chromophotographs? Hundreds perhaps. For all that, Cézanne marks a change—the birth of a movement if not of a slope.

expressing it with primitive sensibility and passion. The last to be infected was one of the finest; and in the eleventh century Norman power and French intelligence produced in the West of Europe a manifestation of the Christian ferment only a little inferior to that which five hundred years earlier had made glorious the East.

Let me insist once again that, when I speak of the Christian ferment or the Christian slope, I am not thinking of dogmatic religion. I am thinking of that religious spirit of which Christianity, with its dogmas and rituals, is one manifestation, Buddhism another. And when I speak of art as a manifestation of the religious spirit I do not mean that art expresses particular religious emotions, much less that it expresses anything theological. I have said that if art expresses anything, it expresses an emotion felt for pure form and that which gives pure form its extraordinary significance. So, when I speak of Christian art, I mean that this art was one product of that state of enthusiasm of which the Christian Church is another. So far was the new spirit from being a mere ebullition of Christian faith that we find manifestations of it in Mohammedan art; everyone who has seen a photograph of the Mosque of Omar at Jerusalem knows that. The emotional renaissance in Europe was not the wide-spreading of Christian doctrines, but it was through Christian doctrine that Europe came to know of the rediscovery of the emotional significance of the Universe. Christian art is not an expression of specific Christian emotions; but it was only when men had been roused by Christianity that they began to feel the emotions that express themselves in form. It was Christianity that put Europe into that state of emotional turmoil from which sprang Christian art.

For a moment, in the sixth century, the flood of enthusiasm seems to have carried the Eastern world, even the official world, off its feet. But Byzantine officials were no fonder of swimming than others. The men who worked the imperial machine, studied the Alexandrine poets, and dabbled in classical archaeology were not the men to look forward. Only the people, led by the monks, were vaguely,

and doubtless stupidly, on the side of emotion and the
future. Soon after Justinian's death the Empire began to
divide itself into two camps. Appropriately, religious art
was the standard of the popular party, and around that
standard the battle raged. "No man," said Lord Melbourne,
"has more respect for the Christian religion than I; but
when it comes to dragging it into private life . . ." At
Constantinople they began dragging religion, and art too,
into the sanctity of private capital. Now, no official worth
his salt can watch the shadow being recklessly sacrificed
to the substance without itching to set the police on some-
body; and the vigilance and sagacity of Byzantine civilians
has become proverbial. We learn from a letter written by
Pope Gregory II to the Emperor Leo, the iconoclast, that
men were willing to give their estates for a picture. This,
to Pope, Emperor, and Mr. Finlay the historian, was
proof enough of appalling demoralisation. For a parallel,
I suppose, they recalled the shameful imprudence of the
Magdalene. There were people at Constantinople who
took art seriously, though in a rather too literary spirit—
"dicunt enim artem pictoriam piam esse." This sort of
thing had to be stopped. Early in the eighth century began
the iconoclast onslaught. The history of that hundred
years' war, in which the popular party carried on a spirited
and finally successful resistance, does not concern us. One
detail, however, is worth noticing. During the iconoclast
persecution a new popular art makes its appearance in
and about those remote monasteries that were the strong-
holds of the mystics. Of this art the Chloudof Psalter is
the most famous example. Certainly the art of the Chloudof
Psalter is not great. A desire to be illustrative generally
mars both the drawing and the design. It mars, but does
not utterly ruin; in many of the drawings something significant persists. There is, however, always too much
realism and too much literature. But neither the realism
nor the literature is derived from classical models. The
work is essentially original. It is also essentially popular.
Indeed, it is something of a party pamphlet; and in one
place we see the Emperor and his cabinet doing duty as

a conclave of the damned. It would be easy to overrate the artistic value of the Chloudof Psalter, but as a document it is of the highest importance, because it brings out clearly the opposition between the official art of the iconoclasts that leaned on the Hellenistic tradition and borrowed bluntly from Bagdad, and the vital art that drew its inspiration from the Christian movement and transmuted all its borrowing into something new. Side by side with this live art of the Christian movement we shall see a continuous output of work based on the imitation of classical models. Those coarse and dreary objects that crop up more or less frequently in early Byzantine, Merovingian, Carolingian, Ottonian, Romanesque, and early Italian art, are not, however, an inheritance from the iconoclastic period; they are the long shadow thrown across history by the gigantic finger of imperial Rome. The mischief done by the iconoclasts was not irreparable, but it was grave. True to their class, Byzantine officials indulged a taste for furniture, giving thereby an unintentional sting to their attack. Like the grandees of the Classical Renaissance, they degraded art, which is a religion, to upholstery, a menial trade. They patronised craftsmen who looked not into their hearts, but into the past—who from the court of the Kalif brought pretty patterns, and from classical antiquity elegant illusions, to do duty for significant design. They looked to Greece and Rome as did the men of the Renaissance; and, like them, lost in the science of representation the art of creation. In the age of the iconoclasts, modelling—the coarse Roman modelling—begins to bulge and curl luxuriously at Constantinople. The eighth century in the East is a portent of the sixteenth in the West. It is the restoration of materialism with its paramour, obsequious art. The art of the iconoclasts tells us the story of their days; it is descriptive, official, eclectic, historical, plutocratic, palatial, and vulgar. Fortunately, its triumph was partial and ephemeral.

For art was still too vigorous to be strangled by a pack of cultivated mandarins. In the end the mystics triumphed. Under the Regent Theodora (842) the images were finally restored; under the Basilian dynasty (867-1057) and under the Comneni Byzantine art enjoyed a second golden age. And though I cannot ~~rate the best Byzantine art of the ninth, tenth, eleventh, and twelfth centuries quite so high as I rate that of the sixth, I am inclined to hold it superior, not only to anything that was to come, but also to the very finest achievement of the greatest ages of Egypt, Crete, and Greece.~~

2. GREATNESS AND DECLINE

HAVING glanced at the beginnings of Christian art, we must not linger over the history of Byzantine. Eastern traders and artisans, pushing into Western Europe from the Adriatic and along the valley of the Rhone, carried with them the ferment. Monks driven out of the East by the iconoclast persecutions found Western Europe Christian and left it religious. The strength of the movement in Europe between 500 and 900 is commonly underrated. That is partly because its extant monuments are not obvious. Buildings are the things to catch the eye, and, outside Ravenna, there is comparatively little Christian architecture of this period. Also the cultivated, spoon-fed art of the renaissance court of Charlemagne is too often allowed to misrepresent one age and disgust another. Of course the bulk of those opulent knick-knacks manufactured for the Carolingian and Ottonian Emperors, and now to be seen at Aachen, are as beastly as anything else that is made simply to be precious. They reflect German taste at its worst; and, in tracing the line, or estimating the value, of the Christian slope it is prudent to overlook even the best of Teutonic effort.[1] For the bulk of it is not primitive or mediaeval or renaissance art, but German art. At any rate it is a manifestation of national character rather than of aesthetic inspiration. Most aesthetic creation bears the mark of nationality; very few manifestations of

---

[1] It will be found instructive to study cases 10-14 of enamels and metal-work at South Kensington. The tyro will have no difficulty in "spotting" the German and Rheinish productions. Alas! the only possible mistake would be a confusion between German and English. Certainly the famous Gloucester candlestick (1100) is as common as anything in the place, unless it be the even more famous Cologne Reliquary (1170).

German nationality bear a trace of aesthetic creation. The
differences between the treasures of Aachen, early German
architecture, fifteenth-century German sculpture, and the
work produced to-day at Munich are superficial. Almost
all is profoundly German, and nothing else. That is to say,
it is conscientious, rightly intentioned, excessively able,
and lacking in just that which distinguishes a work of art
from everything else in the world. The inspiration and
sensibility of the dark ages can be felt most surely and
most easily in the works of minor art produced in France
and Italy.[1] In Italy, however, there is enough architecture
to prove up to the hilt, were further proof required, that
the spirit was vigorous. It is the age of what Sig. Rivoira
calls Pre-Lombardic Architecture—Italian Byzantine: it is
the age of the Byzantine school of painting at Rome.[2]

What the "Barbarians" did, indirectly, for art cannot
be over-estimated. They almost extinguished the tradition
of culture, they began to destroy the bogey of imperialism,
they cleaned the slate. They were able to provide new
bottles for the new wine. Artists can scarcely repress their
envy when they hear that academic painters and masters
were sold into slavery by the score. The Barbarians handed
on the torch and wrought marvels in its light. But in those
days men were too busy fighting and ploughing and pray-
ing to have much time for anything else. Material needs
absorbed their energies without fattening them; their spiritual appetite was ferocious, but they had a live religion
as well as a live art to satisfy it. It is supposed that in the
dark ages insecurity and want reduced humanity to something little better than bestiality. To this their art alone
gives the lie, and there is other evidence. If turbulence and
insecurity could reduce people to bestiality, surely the
Italians of the ninth century were the men to roar and
bleat. Constantly harassed by Saracens, Hungarians, Greeks,

[1] Patriots can take pleasure in the study of Saxon sculpture.
[2] Several schools of painting and drawing flourished during
these centuries in Italy and north of the Alps. In S. Clemente
alone it is easy to discover the work of two distinct periods
between 600 and 900. The extant examples of both are superb.

French, and every sort of German, they had none of those encouragements to labour and create which in the vast security of the *pax Romana* and the *pax Britannica* have borne such glorious fruits of private virtue and public magnificence. Yet in 898 Hungarian scouts report that northern Italy is thickly populated and full of fortified towns.[1] At the sack of Parma (924) forty-four churches were burnt, and these churches were certainly more like Santa Maria di Pomposa or San Pietro at Toscanella than the Colosseum or the Royal Courts of Justice. That the artistic output of the dark ages was to some extent limited by its poverty is not to be doubted; nevertheless, more first-rate art was produced in Europe between the years 500 and 900 than was produced in the same countries between 1450 and 1850.

For in estimating the artistic value of a period one tends first to consider the splendour of its capital achievements. After that one reckons the quantity of first-rate work produced. Lastly, one computes the proportion of undeniable works of art to the total output. In the dark ages the proportion seems to have been high. This is a characteristic of primitive periods. The market is too small to tempt a crowd of capable manufacturers, and the conditions of life are too severe to support the ordinary academy or salon exhibitor who lives on his private means and takes to art because he is unfit for anything else. This sort of producer, whose existence tells us less about the state of art than about the state of society, who would be the worst navvy in his gang or the worst trooper in his squadron, and is the staple product of official art schools, is unheard of in primitive ages. In drawing inferences, therefore, we must not overlook the advantage enjoyed by barbarous periods in the fact that of those who come forward as artists the vast majority have some real gift. I would hazard a guess that of the works that survive from the dark age as high a proportion as one in twelve has real artistic value. Were a proportion of the work produced between 1450 and 1850 identical with that of the work

[1] *The Making of Western Europe*: C. L. R. Fletcher.

produced between 500 and 900 to survive, it might very
well happen that it would not contain a single work of
art. In fact, we tend to see only the more important things
of this period and to leave unvisited the notorious trash.
Yet judging from the picked works brought to our notice
in galleries, exhibitions, and private collections, I cannot
believe that more than one in a hundred of the works
produced between 1450 and 1850 can be properly described
as a work of art.

Between 900 and 1200 the capital achievements of
Christian art are not superior in quality to those of the
preceding age—indeed, they fall short of the Byzantine
masterpieces of the sixth century; but the first-rate art of
this second period was more abundant, or, at any rate,
has survived more successfully, than that of the first. The
age that has bequeathed us Romanesque, Lombardic, and
Norman architecture gives no sign of dissolution. We are
still on the level heights of the Christian Renaissance.
Artists are still primitive. Men still feel the significance of
form sufficiently to create it copiously. Increased wealth
purchases increased leisure, and some of that leisure is
devoted to the creation of art. I do not marvel, therefore,
at the common, though I think inexact, opinion that this
was the period in which Christian Europe touched the
summit of its spiritual history: its monuments are everywhere majestic before our eyes. Not only in France, Italy,
and Spain, but in England, and as far afield as Denmark,
Norway, and Sweden, we can see the triumphs of Romanesque art. This was the last level stage on the long journey
from Santa Sophia to St. John's Wood.

With Gothic architecture the descent began. Gothic
architecture is juggling in stone and glass. It is the con-
voluted road that ends in a bridecake or a cucumber frame.
A Gothic cathedral is a *tour de force;* it is also a melodrama. Enter, and you will be impressed by the incredible
skill of the constructor; perhaps you will be impressed
by a sense of dim mystery and might; you will not be
moved by pure form. You may groan "A-a-h" and collapse:
you will not be strung to austere ecstasy. Walk round it,

and take your pleasure in subtleties of the builder's craft, quaint corners, gargoyles, and flying buttresses, but do not expect the thrill that answers the perception of sheer rightness of form. In architecture the new spirit first came to birth; in architecture first it dies.

We find the spirit alive at the very end of the twelfth century in Romanesque sculpture and in stained glass: we can see it at Chartres and at Bourges. At Bourges there is an indication of the way things are going in the fact that in an unworthy building we find glass and some fragments of sculpture worthy of Chartres, and not unworthy of any age or place. Cimabue and Duccio are the last great exponents in the West of the greater tradition—the tradition that held the essential everything and the accidental nothing. For with Duccio, at any rate, the sense of form was as much traditional as vital: and the great Cimabue is *fin de siècle*. They say that Cimabue died in 1302; Duccio about fifteen years later. With Giotto (born 1276), a greater artist than either, we turn a corner as sharp as that which had been turned a hundred years earlier with the invention of Gothic architecture in France. For Giotto could be intentionally second-rate. He was capable of sacrificing form to drama and anecdote. He never left the essential out, but he sometimes knocked its corners off. He was always more interested in art than in St. Francis, but he did not always remember that St. Francis has nothing whatever to do with art. In theory that is right enough; the Byzantines had believed that they were more interested in dogmatic theology than in form, and almost every great artist has had some notion of the sort. Indeed, it seems that there is nothing so dangerous for an artist as consciously to care about nothing but art. For an artist to believe that his art is concerned with religion or politics or morals or psychology or scientific truth is well; it keeps him alive and passionate and vigorous: it keeps him up out of sentimental aestheticism: it keeps to hand a suitable artistic problem. But for an artist not to be able to forget all about these things as easily as a man who is playing a salmon forgets his lunch is the devil

Giotto lacked facility in forgetting. There are frescoes in which, failing to grasp the significance of a form, he allows it to state a fact or suggest a situation. Giotto went higher than Cimabue but he often aimed lower. Compare his "Virgin and Child" in the Accademia with that of Cimabue in the same gallery, and you will see how low his humanism could bring him. The coarse heaviness of the forms of that woman and her baby is unthinkable in Cimabue; for Cimabue had learnt from the Byzantines that forms should be significant and not life-like. Doubtless in the minds of both there was something besides a preoccupation with formal combinations; but Giotto has allowed that "something" to dominate his design, Cimabue has forced his design to dominate it. There is something protestant about Giotto's picture. He is so dreadfully obsessed by the idea that the humanity of the mother and child is the important thing about them that he has insisted on it to the detriment of his art. Cimabue was incapable of such commonness. Therefore make the comparison—it is salutary and instructive; and then go to Santa Croce or the Arena Chapel and admit that if the greatest name in European painting is not Cézanne it is Giotto.

From the peak that is Giotto the road falls slowly but steadily. Giotto heads a movement towards imitation and scientific picture-making. A genius such as his was bound to be the cause of a movement; it need not have been the cause of such a movement. But the spirit of an age is stronger than the echoes of tradition, sound they never so sweetly. And the spirit of that age, as every extension lecturer knows, moved towards Truth and Nature, away from supernatural ecstasies. There is a moment at which the spirit begins to crave for Truth and Nature, for naturalism and verisimilitude; in the history of art it is known as the early decadence. Nevertheless, on naturalism and materialism a constant war is waged by one or two great souls athirst for pure aesthetic rapture; and this war, strangely enough, is invariably described by the extension lecturer as a fight for Truth and Nature. Never doubt it, in a hundred years or less they will be telling their pupils that in an age of extreme artificiality arose two men, Cézanne and Gauguin, who, by simplicity and sincerity, led back the world to the haunts of Truth and Nature. Strangest of all, some part of what they say will be right.

The new movement broke up the great Byzantine tradition,[1] and left the body of art a victim to the onslaught of that strange, new disease, the Classical Renaissance. The tract that lies between Giotto and Lionardo is the beginning of the end; but it is not the end. Painting came to maturity late, and died hard; and the art of the fourteenth and fifteenth centuries—especially the Tuscan schools—is not a mere historical link: it is an important movement, or rather two. The great Sienese names, Ugolino, Ambrogio Lorenzetti,[2] and Simone Martini, belong to the old world as much as to the new; but the movement that produced Masaccio, Masolino, Castagno, Donatello, Piero della Francesca, and Fra Angelico is a reaction from the Giottesque tradition of the fourteenth century, and an extremely vital movement. Often, it seems, the stir and excitement provoked by the ultimately disastrous scientific discoveries were a cause of good art. It was the disinterested adoration of perspective, I believe, that enabled Uccello and the Paduan Mantegna to apprehend form passionately. The artist must have something to get into a passion about.

Outside Italy, at the beginning of the thirteenth century, the approaches of spiritual bankruptcy are more obvious, though here, too, painting makes a better fight than architecture. Seven hundred years of glorious and incessant creation seem to have exhausted the constructive genius of Europe. Gothic architecture becomes something so nause-

---

[1] Throughout the whole primitive and middle period, however, two tendencies are distinguishable—one vital, derived from Constantinople, the other, dead and swollen, from imperial Rome. Up to the thirteenth century the Byzantine influence is easily predominant. I have often thought that an amusing book might be compiled in which the two tendencies would be well distinguished and illustrated. In Pisa and its neighbourhood the author will find a surfeit of Romanised primitives.

[2] Pietro is, of course, nearer to Giotto.

ous[1] that one can only rejoice when, in the sixteenth century, the sponge is thrown up for good, and, abandoning all attempt to create, Europe settles down quietly to imitate classical models. All true creation was dead long before that; its epitaph had been composed by the master of the "Haute Œuvre" at Beauvais. Only intellectual invention dragged on a sterile and unlucky existence. A Gothic church of the late Middle Ages is a thing made to order. A building formula has been devised within which the artificer, who has ousted the artist, finds endless opportunity for displaying his address. The skill of the juggler and the taste of the pastrycook are in great demand now that the power to feel and the genius to create have been lost. There is brisk trade in pretty things; buildings are stuck all over with them. Go and peer at each one separately if you have a tooth for cheap sweet-meats.

Painting, outside Italy, was following more deliberately the road indicated by architecture. In illuminated manuscripts it is easy to watch the steady coarsening of line and colour. By the beginning of the fourteenth century, Limoges enamels have fallen into that state of damnation from which they have never attempted to rise. Of trans-Alpine figuration after 1250 the less said the better. If in Italian painting the slope is more gentle, that is partly because the spirit of the Byzantine renaissance died harder there, partly because the descent was broken by individual artists who rose superior to their circumstances. But here, too, intellect is filling the void left by emotion; science and culture are doing their work. By the year 1500 the stream of inspiration had grown so alarmingly thin that there was only just enough to turn the wheels of the men of genius. The minor artists seem already prepared to resign themselves to the inevitable. Since we are no longer artists who move, let us be craftsmen who astonish. 'Tis a fine thing to tempt urchins with painted apples: that makes the people stare. To be sure, such feats are rather beneath the

[1] Owing to the English invention of "Perpendicular," the least unsatisfactory style of Gothic architecture, the English find it hard to realise the full horrors of late Gothic.

descendants of Giotto; we leave them to the ~~Dutchmen,~~ whom we envy a little all the same. ~~We have lost art; let us study the science of imitation. Here is a field for learning and dexterity.~~ And, as our patrons who have lost their aesthetic perceptions have not lost all their senses, let us flatter them with grateful objects: let our grapes and girls be as luscious as lifelike. But the patrons are not all sensualists; some of them are scholars. The trade in imitations of the antique is almost as good as the trade in imitations of nature. Archaeology and connoisseurship, those twin ticks on palsied art, are upon us. To react to form a man needs sensibility; to know whether rules have been respected knowledge of these rules alone is necessary. ~~By the end of the fifteenth century art is becoming a question of rules; appreciation a matter of connoisseurship.~~

~~Literature is never pure art.~~ Very little literature is a pure expression of emotion; none, ~~I think is an expression of pure inhuman emotion.~~ Most of it is concerned, to some extent, with facts and ideas: it is intellectual. Therefore literature is a misleading guide to the history of art. Its history is the history of literature; and it is a good guide to the history of thought. Yet sometimes literature will provide the historian of art with a pretty piece of collateral evidence. For instance, the fact that Charles the Great ordained that the Frankish songs should be collected and written down makes a neat pendant to the renaissance art of Aachen. People who begin to collect have lost the first fury of creation. The change that came over plastic art in France towards the end of the twelfth century is reflected in the accomplished triviality of Chrétien de Troyes. The eleventh century had produced the *Chanson de Roland,* a poem as grand and simple as a Romanesque church. Chrétien de Troyes melted down the massive conceptions of his betters and twisted them into fine-spun conceits. He produced a poem as pinnacled, deft, and insignificant as Rouen Cathedral. ~~In literature, as in the visual arts, Italy held out longest, and, when she fell, fell like Lucifer, never to rise again.~~ In Italy there was no literary renaissance; there was just a stirring of the

rubbish heap. If ever man was a full-stop, that man was
Boccaccio. ~~Dante died at Ravenna in 1321.~~ His death is a
landmark in the spiritual history of Europe. Behind him
lies that which, taken with the *Divina Commedia,* has won
for Italy an exaggerated literary reputation. In the thirteenth century there was plenty of poetry hardly inferior
to the *Lamento* of Rinaldo; in the fourteenth comes Pe-
trarch with the curse of mellifluous phrase-making.

May God forget me if I forget the great Italian art of
the fifteenth century. But, a host of individual geniuses
and a cloud of admirable painters notwithstanding, the art
of the fifteenth century was further from grace than that
of the Giottesque painters of the fourteenth. And the whole
output of the ~~fourteenth and fifteenth centuries~~ is im-
measurably inferior to the great ~~Byzantine and Romanesque~~
production of the eleventh and twelfth. ~~Indeed, it is inferior in quality, if not in quantity, to the decadent Byzantine and Italian Byzantine of the thirteen~~th. Therefore
I will say that, already at the end of the fourteenth century,
though Castagno and Masolino and Gentile da Fabriano
and Fra Angelico were alive, and Masaccio and Piero and
Bellini had yet to be born, it looked as if the road that
started from Constantinople in the sixth century were
about to end in a glissade. From Buda-Pest to Sligo, "late
Gothic" stands for something as foul almost as "revival."
Having come through the high passes, Europe, it seemed,
was going to end her journey by plunging down a precipice.
Perhaps it would have been as well; but it was not to be.
The headlong rush was to be checked. The descent was
to be eased by a strange detour, by a fantastic adventure,
a revival that was no re-birth, a Medea's cauldron rather,
an extravagant disease full of lust and laughter; the life
of the old world was to be prolonged by four hundred
years or so, by the galvanising power of the ~~Classical
Renaissance~~.

3. THE CLASSICAL RENAISSANCE AND ITS DISEASES

THE Classical Renaissance is nothing more than a big kink in the long slope; but it is a very big one. ~~It is an intellectual event.~~ Emotionally the consumption that was wasting Europe continued to run its course; the Renaissance was a mere fever-flash. ~~To literature, however, its importance is immense; for literature can make itself independent of spiritual health, and is as much concerned with ideas as with emotions.~~ Literature can subsist in dignity on ideas. Finlay's history of the Byzantine Empire provokes no emotion worth talking about, yet I would give Mr. Finlay a place amongst men of letters, and I would do as much for Hobbes, Mommsen, Sainte-Beuve, Samuel Johnson, and Aristotle. Great thinking without great feeling will make great literature. It is not for their emotional qualities that we value many of our most valued books. And when it is for an emotional quality, to what extent is that emotion aesthetic? I know how little the intellectual and factual content of great poetry has to do with its significance. The actual meaning of the words in Shakespeare's songs, the purest poetry in English, is generally either trivial or trite. They are nursery-rhymes or drawing-room ditties;—

> "Come away, come away, death,
>   And in sad cypress let me be laid;
> Fly away, fly away, breath;
>   I am slain by a fair cruel maid."

Could anything be more commonplace?

> "Hark, hark!
>   Bow, wow,
>   The watch-dogs bark;
>   Bow, wow,
>   Hark, hark! I hear
> The strain of strutting chanticleer
>   Cry, Cock-a-diddle-dow!"

What could be more nonsensical? In the verse of our second poet, Milton—so great that before his name the word "second" rings false as the giggle of fatuity—the ideas are frequently shallow and the facts generally false. In Dante, if the ideas are sometimes profound and the emotions awful, they are also, as a rule, repugnant to our better feelings: the facts are the hoardings of a parish scold. In great poetry it is the formal music that makes the miracle. The poet expresses in verbal form an emotion but distantly related to the words set down. But it is related; it is not a purely artistic emotion. In poetry form and its significance are not everything; the form and the content are not one. Though some of Shakespeare's songs approach purity, there is, in fact, an alloy. The form is burdened with an intellectual content, and that content is a mood that mingles with and reposes on the emotions of life. That is why poetry, though it has its raptures, does not transport us to that remote aesthetic beatitude in which, freed from humanity, we are upstayed by musical and pure visual form.

The Classical Renaissance was a new reading of human life, and what it added to the emotional capital of Europe was a new sense of the excitingness of human affairs. If the men and women of the Renaissance were moved by Art and Nature, that was because in Art and Nature they saw their own reflections. The Classical Renaissance was not a re-birth but a re-discovery; and that superb mess of thought and observation, lust, rhetoric, and pedantry, that we call Renaissance literature, is its best and most characteristic monument. What it re-discovered were the ideas from the heights of which the ancients had gained a view of life. This view the Renaissance borrowed. By doing so it took the sting out of the spiritual death of the late Middle Ages. It showed men that they could manage very well without a soul. It made materialism tolerable by showing how much can be done with matter and intellect. That was its great feat. It taught men how to make the best of a bad job; it proved that by cultivating the senses and setting the intellect to brood over them it is easy to whip up an emotion of sorts. When men had lost sight of the spirit it covered the body with a garment of glamour.

That the Classical Renaissance was essentially an intellectual movement is proved, I think, by the fact that it left the uneducated classes untouched almost. They suffered from its consequences; it gave them nothing. A wave of emotion floods the back-gardens; an intellectual stream is kept within the irrigation channels. The Classical Renaissance made absolute the divorce of the classes from the masses. The mediaeval lord in his castle and the mediaeval hind in his hut were spiritual equals who thought and felt alike, held the same hopes and fears, and shared, to a surprising extent, the pains and pleasures of a simple and rather cruel society. The Renaissance changed all that. The lord entered the new world of ideas and refined sensuality; the peasant stayed where he was, or, as the last vestiges of spiritual religion began to disappear with the commons, sank lower. Popular art changed so gradually that in the late fifteenth and in the sixteenth century we still find, in remote corners, things that are rude but profoundly moving. Village masons could still create in stone at the time when Jacques Cœur was building himself the first "residence worthy of a millionaire" that had been "erected" since the days of Honorius. But that popular art pursued the downhill road sedately while plutocratic art went with a run is a curious accident of which the traces are soon lost; the outstanding fact is that with the Renaissance Europe definitely turns her back on the spiritual view of life. With that renunciation the power of creating significant form becomes the inexplicable gift of the occasional genius. Here and there an individual produces a work of art, so art comes to be regarded as something essentially sporadic and peculiar. The artist is reckoned a freak. We are in the age of names and catalogues and genius-worship. Now, genius-worship is the infallible sign of an uncreative age. In great ages, though we may not all be geniuses, many of us are artists, and where there are many artists art tends to become anonymous.

The Classical Renaissance was something different in kind from what I have called the Christian Renaissance. It must be placed somewhere between 1350 and 1600. Place it where you will. For my part I always think of it as the gorgeous and well-cut garment of the years that fall between 1453 and 1594, between the capture of Constantinople and the death of Tintoretto. To me, it is the age of Lionardo, of Charles VIII and Francis I, of Cesare Borgia and Leo X, of Raffael, of Machiavelli, and of Erasmus, who carries us on to the second stage, the period of angry ecclesiastical politics, of Clement VII, Fontainebleau, Rabelais, Titian, Palladio, and Vasari. But, on any computation, in the years that lie between the spiritual exaltation of the early twelfth century and the sturdy materialism of the late sixteenth lies the Classical Renaissance. Whatever happened, happened between those dates. And all that did happen was nothing more than a change from late manhood to early senility complicated by a house-moving, bringing with it new hobbies and occupations. The decline from the eleventh to the seventeenth century is continuous and to be foreseen; the change from the world of Aurelian to the world of Gregory the Great is catastrophic. Since the Christian Renaissance, new ideas and knowledge notwithstanding, the world has grown rotten with decency and order. It takes more than the rediscovery of Greek texts and Graeco-Roman statues to provoke the cataclysms and earthquakes with which it grew young.

The art of the High Renaissance was conditioned by the demands of its patrons. There is nothing odd about that; it is a recognised stage in the rake's progress. The patrons of the Renaissance wanted plenty of beauty of the kind dear to the impressionable stock-jobber. Only, the plutocrats of the sixteenth century had a delicacy and magnificence of taste which would have made the houses and manners of modern stock-jobbers intolerable to them. Renaissance millionaires could be vulgar and brutal, but they were great gentlemen. They were neither illiterate cads nor meddlesome puritans, nor even saviours of society. Yet, if we are to understand the amazing popularity of Titian's and of Veronese's women, we must take note of their niceness to kiss and obvious willingness to be kissed. That beauty for which can be substituted the word "desirableness," and that insignificant beauty which is the beauty of gems, were in great demand. Imitation was wanted, too; for if pictures are to please as suggestions and mementoes, the objects that suggest and remind must be adequately portrayed. These pictures had got to stimulate the emotions of life, first; aesthetic emotion was a secondary matter. A Renaissance picture was meant to say just those things that a patron would like to hear. That way lies the end of art: however wicked it may be to try to shock the public, it is not so wicked as trying to please it. But whatever the Italian painters of the Renaissance had to say they said in the grand manner. Remember, we are not Dutchmen. Therefore let all your figures suggest the appropriate emotion by means of the appropriate gesture—the gesture consecrated by the great tradition. Straining limbs, looks of love, hate, envy, fear and horror, up-turned or downcast eyes, hands outstretched or clasped in despair—by means of our marvellous machinery, and still more marvellous skill, we can give them all they ask without forestalling the photographers. But we are not recounters all, for some of our patrons are poets. To them the visible Universe is suggestive of moods or, at any rate, sympathetic with them. These value objects for their association with the fun and folly and romance of life. For them, too, we paint pictures, and in their pictures we lend Nature enough humanity to make her interesting. My lord is lascivious? Correggio will give him a background to his mood. My lord is majestic?

Michelangelo will tell him that man is, indeed, a noble animal whose muscles wriggle heroically as watch-springs. The sixteenth century produced a race of artists peculiar in their feeling for material beauty, but normal, coming as they do at the foot of the hills, in their technical proficiency and aesthetic indigence. Craft holds the candle that betrays the bareness of the cupboard. The aesthetic significance of form is feebly and impurely felt, the power of creating it is lost almost; but finer descriptions have rarely been painted. They knew how to paint in the sixteenth century: as for the primitives—God bless them— they did their best: what more could they do when they couldn't even round a lady's thighs?

The Renaissance was a re-birth of other things besides a taste for round limbs and the science of representing them; we begin to hear again of two diseases, endemic in imperial Rome, from which a lively and vigorous society keeps itself tolerably free—Rarity-hunting and Expertise. These parasites can get no hold on a healthy body; it is on dead and dying matter that they batten and grow fat. The passion to possess what is scarce, and nothing else, is a disease that develops as civilisation grows old and dogs it to the grave: it is saprophytic. The rarity-hunter may be called a "collector" if by "collector" you do not mean one who buys what pleases or moves him. Certainly, such an one is unworthy of the name; he lacks the true magpie instinct. To the true collector the intrinsic value of a work of art is irrelevant; the reasons for which he prizes a picture are those for which a philatelist prizes a postage-stamp. To him the question "Does this move me?" is ludicrous: the question "Is it beautiful?"—otiose. Though by the very tasteful collector of stamps or works of art beauty is allowed to be a fair jewel in the crown of rarity, he would have us understand from the first that the value it gives is purely adventitious and depends for its existence on rarity. No rarity, no beauty. As for the profounder aesthetic significance, if a man were to believe in its existence he would cease to be a collector. The question to be asked is—"Is this rare?" Suppose the answer favourable, there remains another—"Is it genuine?" If the work of any particular artist is not rare, if the supply meets the demand, it stands to reason that the work is of no great consequence. For good art is art that fetches good prices, and good prices come of a limited supply. But though it be notorious that the work of Velasquez is comparatively scarce and therefore good, it has yet to be decided whether the particular picture offered at fifty thousand is really the work of Velasquez.

Enter the Expert, whom I would distinguish from the archaeologist and the critic. The archaeologist is a man with a foolish and dangerous curiosity about the past: I am a bit of an archaeologist myself. Archaeology is dangerous because it may easily overcloud one's aesthetic sensibility. The archaeologist may, at any moment, begin to value a work of art not because it is good, but because it is old or interesting. Though that is less vulgar than valuing it because it is rare and precious it is equally fatal to aesthetic appreciation. But so long as I recognise the futility of my science, so long as I recognise that I cannot appreciate a work of art the better because I know when and where it was made, so long as I recognise that, in fact, I am at a certain disadvantage in judging a sixth-century mosaic compared with a person of equal sensibility who knows and cares nothing about Romans and Byzantines, so long as I recognise that art criticism and archaeology are two different things, I hope I may be allowed to dabble unrebuked in my favourite hobby: I hope I am harmless.

Art criticism, in the present state of society, seems to me a respectable and possibly a useful occupation. The prejudice against critics, like most prejudices, lives on fear and ignorance. It is quite unnecessary and rather provincial, for, in fact, critics are not very formidable. They are suspected of all sorts of high-handed practices—making and breaking reputations, running up and down, booming and exploiting—of which I should hardly think them capable. Popular opinion notwithstanding, I doubt whether critics are either omnipotent or utterly depraved. Indeed, I believe that some of them are not only blameless but even

lovable characters. Those sinister but flattering insinuations
and open charges of corruption fade woefully when one
considers how little the critic of contemporary art can
hope to get for "writing up" pictures that sell for twenty
or thirty guineas apiece. The expert, to be sure, is exposed
to some temptation, since a few of his words, judiciously
placed, may promote a canvas from the twenty to the
twenty thousand mark; but, as everyone knows, the moral-
ity of the expert is above suspicion. Useless as the occupation of the critic may be, it is probably honest; and, after
all, is it more useless than all other occupations, save
only those of creating art, producing food, drink, and
tobacco, and bearing beautiful children?

If the collector asks me, as a critic, for my opinion of
the Velasquez he is about to buy, I will tell him honestly
what I think of it, as a work of art. I will tell him whether
it moves me much or little, and I will try to point out
those qualities and relations of line and colour in which
it seems to me to excel or fall short. I will try to account
for the degree of my aesthetic emotion. That, I conceive,
is the function of the critic. But all conjectures as to the
authenticity of a work based on its formal significance,
or even on its technical perfection, are extremely hazard-
ous. It is always possible that someone else was the master's
match as artist and craftsman, and of that someone's work
there may be an overwhelming supply. The critic may sell
the collector a common pup instead of the one uncatalogued
specimen of Pseudokuniskos; and therefore the wary collector sends for someone who can furnish him with the
sort of evidence of the authenticity of his picture that
would satisfy a special juryman and confound a purchasing
dealer. At artistic evidence he laughs noisily in half-crown
periodicals and five-guinea tomes. Documentary evidence
is what he prefers; but, failing that, he will put up with a
cunning concoction of dates and water-marks, cabalistic
signatures, craquelure, patina, chemical properties of paint
and medium, paper and canvas, all sorts of collateral
evidence, historical and biographical, and racy tricks of

brush or pen. It is to adduce and discuss this sort of evidence that the Collector calls in the Expert.

Anyone whom chance or misfortune has led into the haunts of collectors and experts will admit that I have not exaggerated the horror of the diseases that we have inherited from the Classical Renaissance. He will have heard the value of a picture made to depend on the interpretation of a letter. He will have heard the picture discussed from every point of view except that of one who feels its significance. By whom was it made? For whom was it made? When was it made? Where was it made? Is it all the work of one hand? Who paid for it? How much did he pay? Through what collections has it passed? What are the names of the figures portrayed? What are their histories? What the style and cut of their coats, breeches, and beards? How much will it fetch at Christie's? All these are questions to moot; and mooted they will be, by the hour. But in expert conclaves who has ever heard more than a perfunctory and silly comment on the aesthetic qualities of a masterpiece?

We have seen the scholars at loggerheads over the genuineness of a picture in the National Gallery. The dispute rages round the interpretation of certain marks in the corner of the canvas. Are they, or are they not, a signature? Whatever the final decision may be, the picture will remain unchanged; but if it can be proved that the marks are the signature of the disciple, it will be valueless. If the Venus of Velasquez should turn out to be a Spanish model by del Mazo, the great ones who guide us and teach the people to love art will see to it, I trust, that the picture is moved to a position befitting its mediocrity. It is this unholy alliance between Expertise and Officialdom [1]

[1] In speaking of officialdom it is not the directors of galleries and departments whom I have in mind. Many of them are on the right side; we should all be delighted to see Sir Charles Holroyd or Mr. Maclagan, for instances, let loose amongst the primitives with forty thousand pounds in pocket. I am thinking of those larger luminaries who set their important faces against the acquisition of works of art, the men who have been put in authority over directors and the rest of us.

that squanders twenty thousand on an unimpeachable Frans
Hals, and forty thousand on a Mabuse for which no minor
artist will wish to take credit.[1] For the money a judicious
purchaser could have made one of the finest collections
in England. The unholy alliance has no use for contemporary art. The supply is considerable and the names are
not historic. Snobbery makes acceptable the portrait of a
great lady, though it be by Boldini; and even Mr. Lavery
may be welcome if he come with the picture of a king.
But how are our ediles to know whether a picture of a
commoner, or of some inanimate and undistinguished object, by Degas or Cézanne is good or bad? They need not
know whether a picture by Hals is good; they need only
know that it is by Hals.

I will not describe in any detail the end of the slope,
from the beginning of the seventeenth to the middle of
the nineteenth century. The seventeenth century is rich
in individual geniuses; but they are individual. The level
of art is very low. The big names of El Greco, Rembrandt,
Velasquez, Vermeer, Rubens, Jordaens, Poussin, and
Claude, Wren and Bernini (as architects) stand out; had
they lived in the eleventh century they might all have been
lost in a crowd of anonymous equals. Rembrandt, indeed,
perhaps the greatest genius of them all, is a typical ruin
of his age. For, except in a few of his later works, his
sense of form and design is utterly lost in a mess of
rhetoric, romance, and chiaroscuro. It is difficult to forgive
the seventeenth century for what it made of Rembrandt's
genius. One great advantage over its predecessor it did
enjoy: the seventeenth century had ceased to believe sin-
cerely in the ideas of the Classical Renaissance. Painters
could not devote themselves to suggesting the irrelevant
emotions of life because they did not feel them.[2] For lack
of human emotion they were driven back on art. They

---

[1] The Mabuse, however, was a bargain that the merchants
and money-lenders who settle these things could hardly be
expected to resist. The ticket price is said to have been
£120,000.
[2] It was Mr. Roger Fry who made this illuminating discovery.

talked a great deal about Magnanimity and Nobility, but they thought more of Composition. For instance, in the best works of Nicolas Poussin, the greatest artist of the age, you will notice that the human figure is treated as a shape cut out of coloured paper to be pinned on as the composition directs. That is the right way to treat the human figure; the mistake lay in making these shapes retain the characteristic gestures of Classical rhetoric. In much the same way Claude treats temples and palaces, trees, mountains, harbours and lakes, as you may see in his superb pictures at the National Gallery. There they hang, beside the Turners, that all the world may see the difference between a great artist and an after-dinner poet. Turner was so much excited by his observations and his sentiments that he set them all down without even trying to co-ordinate them in a work of art: clearly he could not have done so in any case. That was a cheap and spiteful thought that prompted the clause wherein it is decreed that his pictures shall hang for ever beside those of Claude. He wished to call attention to a difference and he has succeeded beyond his expectations: curses, like hens, come home to roost.

In the eighteenth century, with its dearth of genius, we perceive more clearly that we are on the flats. Chardin is the one great artist. Painters are, for the most part, upholsterers to the nobility and gentry. Some fashion handsome furniture for the dining-room, others elegant knickknacks for the boudoir; many are kept constantly busy delineating for the respect of future generations his lordship, or her ladyship's family. The painting of the eighteenth century is brilliant illustration still touched with art. For instance, in Watteau, Canaletto, Crome, Cotman, and Guardi there is some art, some brilliance, and a great deal of charming illustration. In Tiepolo there is hardly anything but brilliance; only when one sees his work beside that of Mr. Sargent does one realise the presence of other qualities. In Hogarth there is hardly anything but illustration; one realises the presence of other qualities only by remembering the work of the Hon. John Collier. Beside the upholsterers who work for the aristocracy there is another class supported by the connoisseurs. There are the conscientious bores, whose modest aim it is to paint and draw correctly in the manner of Raffael and Michelangelo. ~~Their first object is to stick to the rules, their second to show some cleverness in doing so.~~ One need not bother about them.

~~So the power of creating is almost lost, and limners must be content to copy pretty thing~~s. The twin pillars of painting in the eighteenth century were what they called "Subject" and "Treatment." To paint a beautiful picture, a boudoir picture, take a pretty woman, note those things about her that a chaste and civil dinner-partner might note, and set them down in gay colours and masses of Chinese white: you may do the same by her toilette battery, her fancy frocks, and picnic parties. ~~Imitate whatever is pretty and you are sure~~ to make a pretty job of it. To make a noble picture, a dining-room piece, you must take the same lady and invest her in a Doric chiton or diploida and himation; give her a pocillum, a censer, a sacrificial ram, and a distant view of Tivoli; round your modelling, and let your brush-strokes be long and slightly curved; affect sober and rather hot pigments; call the finished article "Dido pouring libations to the Goddess of Love." To paint an exhibition picture, the sort preferred by the more rigid *cognoscenti,* be sure to make no mark for which warrant cannot be found in Rubens, Sarto, Guido Reni, Titian, Tintoretto, Veronese, Raffael, Michelangelo, or Trajan's Column. For further information consult "The Discourses" of Sir Joshua Reynolds, P.R.A., whose recipes are made palatable by a quality infrequent in his dishes, ~~luminosity.~~

The intellectual reaction from Classical to Romantic is duly registered by a change of subject. Ruins and mediaeval history come into fashion. For art, which is as little concerned with the elegant bubbles of the eighteenth century as with the foaming superabundance of the Romantic revival, this change is nothing more than the swing of an irrelevant pendulum. But the new ideas led inevitably to antiquarianism, and antiquarians found something extraordinarily congenial in what was worst in Gothic art. Obedient limners follow the wiseacres. What else is there for them to follow? Stragglers from the age of reason are set down to trick out simpering angels. No longer permitted to stand on the laws of propriety or their personal dignity, they are ordered to sweeten their cold meats with as much amorous and religious sentiment as they can exude. Meanwhile the new fellows, far less sincere than the old, who felt nothing and said so, begin to give themselves the airs of artists. These Victorians are intolerable: for now that they have lost the old craft and the old tradition of taste, the pictures that they make are no longer pleasantly insignificant; they bellow "stinking mackerel."

About the middle of the nineteenth century art was as nearly dead as art can be. The road ran drearily through the sea-level swamps. There were, of course, men who felt that imitation, whether of nature or of another's work, was not enough, who felt the outrage of calling the staple products of the "forties" and "fifties" art; but generally they lacked the power to make an effective protest. Art cannot die out utterly; but it lay sick in caves and cellars. There were always one or two who had a right to call themselves artists: the great Ingres [1] overlaps Crome; Corot and Daumier overlap Ingres; and then come the Impressionists. But the mass of painting and sculpture had sunk to something that no intelligent and cultivated person would dream of calling art. It was in those days that they invented the commodity which is still the staple of official exhibitions throughout Europe. You may see acres of it

---

[1] It is pleasant to remember that by the painters, critics, and rich amateurs of "the old gang" the pictures of Ingres were treated as bad jokes. Ingres was accused of distortion, ugliness, and even of incompetence! His work was called "mad" and "puerile." He was derided as a pseudo-primitive, and hated as one who would subvert the great tradition by trying to put back the clock four hundred years. The same authorities discovered in 1824 that Constable's *Hay Wain* was the outcome of a sponge full of colour having been thrown at a canvas. *Nous avons changé tout ça.*

every summer at Burlington House and in the Salon; indeed, you may see little else there. It does not pretend to
be art. If the producers mistake it for art sometimes,
they do so in all innocence: they have no notion of what
art is. By "art" they mean the imitation of objects, preferably pretty or interesting ones; their spokesmen have said
so again and again. The sort of thing that began to do
duty for art about 1840, and still passes muster with the
lower middle class, would have been inconceivable at any
time between the fall of the Roman Empire and the death
of George IV. Even in the eighteenth century, when they
could not create significant form, they knew that accurate
imitation was of no value in itself. It is not until what is
still official painting and sculpture and architecture gets
itself accepted as a substitute for art, that we can say for
certain that the long slope that began with the Byzantine
primitives is ended. But when we have reached this point
we know that we can sink no lower.

We must mark the spot near which a huge impulse
died; but we need not linger in the fetid swamps—or only
long enough to say a word of justice. Do not rail too
bitterly against official painters, living or dead. They cannot harm art, because they have nothing to do with it:
they are not artists. If rail you must, rail at that public
which, having lost all notion of what art is, demanded,
and still demands, in its stead, the thing that these painters
can supply. Official painting is the product of social conditions which have not yet passed away. Thousands of
people who care nothing about art are able to buy and
are in the habit of buying pictures. They want a background, just as the ladies and gentlemen of the *ancien
régime* wanted one; only their idea of what a background
should be is different. The painter of commerce supplies
what is wanted and in his simplicity calls it art. That it
is not art, that it is not even an amenity, should not blind
us to the fact that it is an honest article. I admit that the
man who produces it satisfies a vulgar and unprofitable
taste; so does the very upright tradesman who forces in-
sipid asparagus for the Christmas market. Sir Georgius

Midas will never care for art, but he will always want a background; and, unless things are going to change with surprising suddenness, it will be some time before he is unable to get what he wants, at a prize. However splendid and vital the new movement may be, it will not, I fancy, unaided, kill the business of picture-making. The trade will dwindle; but I suspect it will survive until there is no one who can afford ostentatious upholstery, until the only purchasers are those who willingly make sacrifices for the joy of possessing a work of art.

4. ALID EX ALIO

IN THE nineteenth century the spirit seems to enter one of those prodigious periods of incubation for a type of which we turn automatically to the age that saw the last infirmity of Roman imperialism and of Hellenistic culture. About Victorian men and movement there is something uneasy. It is as though, having seen a shilling come down "tails," one were suddenly to surprise the ghost of a head—you could have sworn that "heads" it was. It doesn't matter, but it's disquieting. And after all, perhaps it does matter. Seen from odd angles, Victorian judges and ministers take on the airs of conspirators: there is something prophetic about Mr. Gladstone—about the Newcastle programme something pathetic. Respectable hypotheses are caught implying the most disreputable conclusions. And yet the respectable classes speculate, while anarchists and supermen are merely horrified by the card-playing and champagne-drinking of people richer than themselves. Agnostics see the finger of God in the fall of godless Paris. Individualists clamour for a large and vigilant police force.

That is how the nineteenth century looks to us. Most of the mountains are in labour with ridiculous mice, but the spheres are shaken by storms in intellectual tea-cups. The Pre-Raffaelites call in question the whole tradition of the Classical Renaissance, and add a few more names to the heavy roll of notoriously bad painters. The French Impressionists profess to do no more than push the accepted theory of representation to its logical conclusion, and by their practice, not only paint some glorious pictures, but shake the fatal tradition and remind the more intelligent part of the world that visual art has nothing to do with literature. Whistler draws, not the whole, but

125

a part of the true moral. What a pity he was not a greater artist! Still, he was an artist; and about the year 1880 the race was almost extinct in this country.[1]

Through the fog of the nineteenth century, which began in 1830, loom gigantic warnings. All the great figures are ominous. If they do not belong to the new order, they make impossible the old. Carlyle and Dickens and Victor Hugo, the products and lovers of the age, scold it. Flaubert points a contemptuous finger. Ibsen, a primitive of the new world, indicates the cracks in the walls of the old. Tolstoi is content to be nothing but a primitive until he becomes little better than a bore. By minding his own business, Darwin called in question the business of everyone else. By hammering new sparks out of an old instrument, Wagner revealed the limitations of literary music. As the twentieth century dawns, a question, which up to the time of the French Revolution had been judiciously kept academic, shoulders its way into politics: "Why is this good?" About the same time, thanks chiefly to the Aesthetes and the French Impressionists, an aesthetic conscience, dormant since before the days of the Renaissance, wakes and begins to cry, "Is this art?"

It is amusing to remember that the first concerted clamour against the Renaissance and its florid sequelae arose in England; for the Romantic movement, which was as much French and German as English, was merely a reaction from the classicism of the eighteenth century, and hardly attacked, much less threw off, the dominant tyranny. We have a right to rejoice in the Pre-Raffaelite movement as an instance of England's unquestioned supremacy in independence and unconventionality of thought. Depression begins when we have to admit that the revolt led to nothing but a great many bad pictures and a little thin sentiment. The Pre-Raffaelites were men of taste who felt the commonness of the High Renaissance and the distinction of what they called Primitive Art, by which they meant the art of the fifteenth and fourteenth centuries. They saw that, since the Renaissance, painters had been

[1] As Mr. Walter Sickert reminds me, there was Sickert.

trying to do something different from what the primitives had done; but for the life of them they could not see what it was that the primitives did. They had the taste to prefer Giotto to Raffael, but the only genuine reason they could give for their preference was that they felt Raffael to be vulgar. The reason was good, but not fundamental; so they set about inventing others. They discovered in the primitives scrupulous fidelity to nature, superior piety, chaste lives. How far they were from guessing the secret of primitive art appeared when they began to paint pictures themselves. The secret of primitive art is the secret of all art, at all times, in all places—sensibility to the profound significance of form and the power of creation. The band of happy brothers lacked both; so perhaps it is not surprising that they should have found in acts of piety, in legends and symbols, the material, and in sound churchmanship the very essence, of mediaeval art. For their own inspiration they looked to the past instead of looking about them. Instead of diving for truth they sought it on the surface. The fact is, the Pre-Raffaelites were not artists, but archaeologists who tried to make intelligent curiosity do the work of impassioned contemplation. As artists they do not differ essentially from the ruck of Victorian painters. They will reproduce the florid ornament of late Gothic as slavishly as the steady Academician reproduces the pimples on an orange; and if they do attempt to simplify—some of them have noticed the simplification of the primitives—they do so in the spirit, not of an artist, but of the "sedulous ape."

Simplification is the conversion of irrelevant detail into significant form. A very bold Pre-Raffaelite was capable of representing a meadow by two minutely accurate blades of grass. But two minutely accurate blades of grass are just as irrelevant as two million; it is the formal significance of a blade of grass or of a meadow with which the artist is concerned. The Pre-Raffaelite method is at best symbolism, at worst pure silliness. Had the Pre-Raffaelites been blessed with profoundly imaginative minds they might have recaptured the spirit of the Middle Ages instead of

imitating its least significant manifestations. But had they
been great artists they would not have wished to recapture
anything. They would have invented forms for themselves
or derived them from their surroundings, just as the mediaeval artists did. ~~Great artists never look back~~.

When art is as nearly dead as it was in the middle of
the nineteenth century, scientific accuracy is judged the
proper end of painting. Very well, said the ~~French Impressionists, be accurate, be scientific~~. At best the Academic
painter sets down his concepts; but the ~~concept is not a
scientific reality; the men of science tell us that the visible
reality of the Universe is vibrations of light~~. Let us represent things as they are—~~scientifically. Let us represent
light~~. Let us paint what we see, not the intellectual super-
structure that we build over our sensations. That was the
theory: and if the end of art were representation it would
be sound enough. But the end of art is not representation,
as the great Impressionists, Renoir, Degas, Manet, knew
(two of them happily know it still) the moment they left
off arguing and bolted the studio door on that brilliant
theorist, Claude Monet. Some of them, to be sure, turned
out polychromatic charts of desolating dullness—Monet
towards the end, for instance. The Neo-Impressionists—
Seurat, Signac, and Cross—have produced little else. And
any Impressionist, under the influence of Monet and
Watteau, was capable of making a poor, soft, formless
thing. ~~But more often the Impressionist masters, in their
fantastic and quite unsuccessful pursuit of scientific truth,
created works of art tolerable in design and glorious in
colour~~. Of course this oasis in the mid-century desert
delighted the odd people who cared about art; they pre-
tended at first to be absorbed in the scientific accuracy
of the thing, but before long they realised that they were
deceiving themselves, and gave up the pretence. For they
saw very clearly that these pictures differed most profoundly from the anecdotic triumphs of Victorian workshops, not in their respectful attention to scientific theory,
but in the fact that, though they made little or no appeal
to the interests of ordinary life, they provoked a far more

potent and profound emotion. Scientific theories notwithstanding, the Impressionists provoked that emotion which
all great art provokes—an emotion in the existence of
which the bulk of Victorian artists and critics were, for
obvious reasons, unable to believe. The virtue of these
Impressionist pictures, whatever it might be, depended on
no reference to the outside world. What could it be?
"Sheer beauty," said the enchanted spectators. They were
not far wrong.

That beauty is the one essential quality in a work of
art is a doctrine that has been too insistently associated
with the name of Whistler, who is neither its first nor its
last, nor its most capable, exponent—but only of his age
the most conspicuous. To read Whistler's *Ten o'Clock*
will do no one any harm, or much good. It is neither very
brilliant nor at all profound, but it is in the right direction.
Whistler is not to be compared with the great controversial-
ists any more than he is to be compared with the great
artists. To set *The Gentle Art* beside *The Dissertation on
the Letters of Phalaris,* Gibbon's *Vindication,* or the po-
lemics of Voltaire, would be as unjust as to hang "Cremorne
Gardens" in the Arena Chapel. Whistler was not even
cock of the Late Victorian walk; both Oscar Wilde and
Mr. Bernard Shaw were his masters in the art of con-
troversy. But amongst Londoners of the "eighties" he is
a bright figure, as much alone almost in his knowledge of
what art is, as in his power of creating it: and it is this that
gives a peculiar point and poignance to all his quips and
quarrels. There is dignity in his impudence. He is using
his rather obvious cleverness to fight for something dearer
than vanity. He is a lonely artist, standing up and hitting
below the belt for art. To the critics, painters, and sub-
stantial men of his age he was hateful because he was an
artist; and because he knew that their idols were humbugs
he was disquieting. Not only did he have to suffer the
grossness and malice of the most insensitive pack of
butchers that ever scrambled into the seat of authority;
he had also to know that not one of them could by any
means be made to understand one word that he spoke in

seriousness. Overhaul the English art criticism of that time, from the cloudy rhetoric of Ruskin to the journalese of " 'Arry," and you will hardly find a sentence that gives ground for supposing that the writer has so much as guessed what art is. "As we have hinted, the series does not represent any Venice that we much care to remember; for who wants to remember the degradation of what has been noble, the foulness of what has been fair?"—" 'Arry" in the *Times*. No doubt it is becoming in an artist to leave all criticism unanswered; it would be foolishness in a schoolboy to resent stuff of this sort. Whistler replied; and in his replies to ignorance and insensibility, seasoned with malice, he is said to have been ill-mannered and caddish. He was; but in these respects he was by no means a match for his most reputable enemies. And ill-mannered, ill-tempered, and almost alone, he was defending art, while they were flattering all that was vilest in Victorianism.

As I have tried to show in another place, it is not very difficult to find a flaw in the theory that beauty is the essential quality in a work of art—that is, if the word "beauty" be used, as Whistler and his followers seem to have used it, to mean insignificant beauty. It seems that the beauty about which they were talking was the beauty of a flower or a butterfly; now I have very rarely met a person delicately sensitive to art who did not agree, in the end, that a work of art moved him in a manner altogether different from, and far more profound than, that in which a flower or a butterfly moved him. Therefore, if you wish to call the essential quality in a work of art "beauty" you must be careful to distinguish between the beauty of a work of art and the beauty of a flower, or, at any rate, between the beauty that those of us who are not great artists perceive in a work of art and that which the same people perceive in a flower. Is it not simpler to use different words? In any case, the distinction is a real one: compare your delight in a flower or a gem with what you feel before a great work of art, and you will find no difficulty, I think, in differing from Whistler.

Anyone who cares more for a theory than for the truth

is at liberty to say that the art of the ~~Impressionists, with their absurd notions about scientific representation, is a lovely fungus growing very naturally on the ruins of the Christian slope~~. The same can hardly be said about Whistler, who was definitely in revolt against the theory of his age. For we must never forget that accurate representation of what the grocer thinks he sees was the central dogma of Victorian art. It is the general acceptance of this view— ~~that the accurate imitation of objects is an essential quality in a work of art—~~ and the general inability to create, or even to recognise, aesthetic qualities, that mark the nineteenth century as the end of a slope. Except stray artists and odd amateurs, and you may say that in the middle of the nineteenth century art had ceased to exist. That is the importance of the official and academic art of that age: it shows us that we have touched bottom. It has the importance of an historical document. In the eighteenth century there was still a tradition of art. Every official and academic painter, even at the end of the eighteenth century, whose name was known to the cultivated public, whose works were patronised by collectors, knew perfectly ~~well that the end of art was not imitation, that forms must have some aesthetic significance~~. Their successors in the nineteenth century did not. Even the tradition was dead. That means that generally and officially art was dead. We have seen it die. The Royal Academy and the Salon have been made to serve their useful, historical purpose. We need say no more about them. Whether those definitely artistic cliques of the nineteenth century, ~~the men who made form a means to aesthetic emotion and not a means of stating facts and conveying ideas, the Impressionists and the Aesthetes, Manet and Renoir, Whistler and Conder, &c. &c., are to be regarded as accidental flowers blossoming on a grave or as portents of a new age, will depend upon the temperament of him who regards them~~.

But a sketch of the Christian ~~slope may well end with the Impressionists~~, for Impressionist theory is a blind alley. Its only logical development would be an art-machine— a machine for establishing values correctly, and determining what the eye sees scientifically, thereby making the production of art a mechanical certainty. Such a machine, I am told, was invented by an Englishman. Now if the praying-machine be admittedly the last shift of senile religion, the value-finding machine may fairly be taken for the psychopomp of art. Art has passed from the primitive creation of significant form to the highly civilised statement of scientific fact. I think the machine, which is the intelligent and respectable end, should be preserved, if still it exists, at South Kensington or in the Louvre, along with the earlier monuments of the Christian slope. As for that uninteresting and disreputable end, official nineteenth-century art, it can be studied in a hundred public galleries and in annual exhibitions all over the world. It is the mouldy and therefore the obvious end. The spirit that came to birth with the triumph of art over Graeco-Roman realism dies with the ousting of art by the picture of commerce.

But if the Impressionists, with their scientific equipment, their astonishing technique, and their intellectualism, mark the end of one era, do they not rumour the coming of another? Certainly to-day there is stress in the cryptic laboratory of Time. A great thing is dead; but, as that sagacious Roman noted:

> "haud igitur penitus pereunt quaecumque videntur,
>   quando alid ex alio reficit natura nec ullam
>   rem gigni patitur nisi morte adiuta aliena."

And do not the Impressionists, with their power of creating works of art that stand on their own feet, bear in their arms a new age? For if the venial sin of Impressionism is a grotesque theory and its justification a glorious practice, its historical importance consists in its having taught people to seek the significance of art in the work itself, instead of hunting for it in the emotions and interests of the outer world.

IV

THE MOVEMENT

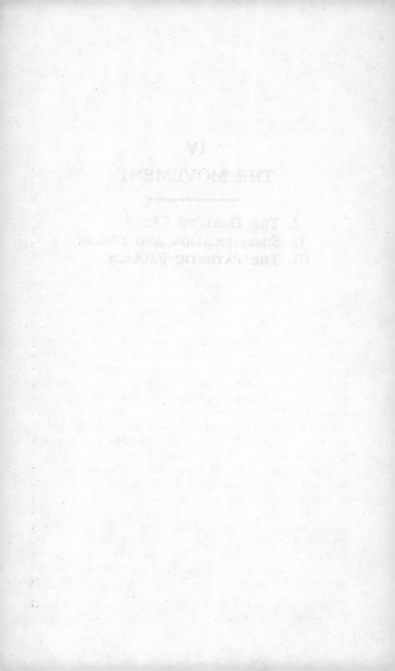

1. THE DEBT TO CÉZANNE

THAT with the maturity of Cézanne a new movement came to birth will hardly be disputed by anyone who has managed to survive the "nineties"; that this movement is the beginning of a new slope is a possibility worth discussing, but about which no decided opinion can yet be held. In so far as one man can be said to inspire a whole age, Cézanne inspires the contemporary movement: he stands a little apart, however, because he is too big to take a place in any scheme of historical development; he is one of those figures that dominate an age and are not to be fitted into any of the neat little pigeon-holes so thoughtfully prepared for us by evolutionists. He passed through the greater part of life unnoticed, and came near creeping out of it undiscovered. No one seems to have guessed at what was happening. It is easy now to see how much we owe to him, and how little he owed to anyone; for us it is easy to see what Gauguin and Van Gogh borrowed—in 1890, the year in which the latter died, it was not so. They were sharp eyes, indeed, that discerned before the dawn of the new century that Cézanne had founded a movement.

That movement is still young. But I think it would be safe to say that already it has produced as much good art as its predecessor. Cézanne, of course, created far greater things than any Impressionist painter; and Gauguin, Van Gogh, Matisse, Rousseau, Picasso, de Vlaminck, Derain, Herbin, Marchand, Marquet, Bonnard, Duncan Grant, Maillol, Lewis, Kandinsky, Brancusi, von Anrep, Roger Fry, Friesz, Goncharova, L'Hôte, are Rolands for the Olivers of any other artistic period.[1] They are not all great

[1] Need I say that this list is not intended to be exhaustive? It is merely representative.

artists, but they all are artists. If the Impressionists raised
the proportion of works of art in the general pictorial output from about one in five hundred thousand to one in a
hundred thousand, the Post-Impressionists (for after all
it is sensible to call the group of vital artists who immediately follow the Impressionists by that name) have
raised the average again. Today, I daresay, it stands as
high as one in ten thousand. Indeed, it is this that has led
some people to see in the new movement the dawn of a
new age; for nothing is more characteristic of a "primitive"
movement than the frequent and widespread production
of genuine art. Another hopeful straw at which the sanguine
catch is the admirable power of development possessed by
the new inspiration. As a rule, the recognition of a movement as a movement is its death. As soon as the pontiffs
discovered Impressionism, some twenty years after its
patent manifestation, they academized it. They set their
faces against any sort of development and drove into revolt
or artistic suicide every student with an ounce of vitality
in him. Before the inspiration of Cézanne had time to
grow stale, it was caught up by such men as Matisse and
Picasso; by them it was moulded into forms that suited
their different temperaments, and already it shows signs
of taking fresh shape to express the sensibility of a younger
generation.[1]

This is very satisfactory but it does not suffice to prove
that the new movement is the beginning of a new slope;
it does not prove that we stand now where the early
Byzantines stood, with the ruins of a civilisation clattering
about our ears and our eyes set on a new horizon. In
favour of that view there are no solid arguments; yet are
there general considerations, worth stating and pondering,
though not to be pushed too violently. He who would cast

[1] Let us hope that it will. There certainly are ominous signs
of academization amongst the minor men of the movement.
There is the beginning of a tendency to regard certain simplifications and distortions as ends in themselves and party
badges. There is some danger of an attempt to impose a
formula on the artist's individuality. At present the infection
has not spread far, and the disease has taken a mild form.

the horoscope of humanity, or of any human activity, must neither neglect history nor trust her overmuch. Certainly the neglect of history is the last mistake into which a modern speculator is likely to fall. To compare Victorian England with Imperial Rome has been the pastime of the half-educated these fifty years. *"Tu regere imperio populos, Romane, memento,"* is about as much Latin as it is becoming in a public schoolman to remember. The historically minded should travel a little further with their comparison (to be sure, some have done so in search of arguments against Socialism); on their way, they will not have failed to remark the materialism, the mechanical cunning, the high standard of comfort, the low standard of honesty, the spiritual indigence, the unholy alliance of cynicism with sentimentality, the degradation of art and religion to menial and mountebank offices, common in both, and in both signifying the mouldy end of what was once a vital agitation. To similise the state superstitions and observances of Rome with our official devotions and ministration, the precise busts in the British Museum with the "speaking likenesses" in the National Portrait Gallery, the academic republicanism of the cultivated patricians with English Liberalism, and the thrills of the arena with those of the playing-field, would be pretty sport for any little German boy. I shall not encourage the brat to lay an historical finger on callousness, bravado, trembling militarism, superficial culture, mean political passion, megalomania, and a taste for being in the majority as attributes common to Imperial Rome and Imperial England. Rather I will inquire whether the rest of Europe does not labour under the proverbial disability of those who live in glass-houses. It is not so much English politics as Western civilisation that reminds me of the last days of the Empire.

The facility of the comparison disfavours the raking up of similarities; I need not compare Mr. Shaw with Lucian or the persecution of Christians with the savage outbursts of our shopkeepers against anarchists. One may note, though, that it is as impossible to determine exactly when and whence came the religious spirit that was to make an end of Graeco-Roman materialism as to assign a birth-place to the spiritual ferment that pervades modern Europe. For though we may find a date for the maturity of Cézanne, and though I agree that the art of one genius may produce a movement, even Cézanne will hardly suffice to account for what looks like the beginning of an artistic slope and a renaissance of the human spirit. One would hesitate to explain the dark and middle ages by the mosaics at Ravenna. The spirit that was to revive the moribund Roman world came from the East; that we know. It was at work long before the world grew conscious of its existence. Its remotest origins are probably undiscoverable. To-day we can name pioneers, beside Cézanne, in the new world of emotion; there was Tolstoi, and there was Ibsen; but who can say that these did not set out in search of Eldorados of which already they had heard travellers' tales. Ruskin shook his fist at the old order to some purpose; and, if he could not see clearly what things counted, succeeded at least in making contemptible some that did not. Nietzsche's preposterous nonsense knocked the bottom out of nonsense more preposterous and far more vile. But to grub for origins is none of my business; when the Church shall be established be sure that industrious hagiographers will do justice to its martyrs and missionaries.

Consider, too, that a great emotional renaissance must be preceded by an intellectual, destructive movement. To that how shall we assign a starting-point? It could be argued, I suppose, that it began with Voltaire and the Encyclopædists. Having gone so far back, the historian would find cause for going further still. How could he justify any frontier? Every living organism is said to carry in itself the germ of its own decay, and perhaps a civilisation is no sooner alive than it begins to contrive its end. Gradually the symptoms of disease become apparent to acute physicians who state the effect without perceiving the cause. Be it so; circular fatalism is as cheerful as it is sad. If ill must follow good, good must follow ill. In any case, I have said enough to show that if Europe be again at the head of a pass, if we are about to take the first step along a new slope, the historians of the new age will have plenty to quarrel about.

It may be because the nineteenth century was preparing Europe for a new epoch, that it understood better its destructive critics than its constructive artists. At any rate before that century ended it had produced one of the great constructive artists of the world, and overlooked him. Whether or no he marks the beginning of a slope, Cézanne certainly marks the beginning of a movement the main characteristics of which it will be my business to describe. For, though there is some absurdity in distinguishing one artistic movement from another, since all works of art, to whatever age they belong, are essentially the same: yet these superficial differences which are the characteristics of a movement have an importance beyond that dubious one of assisting historians. The particular methods of creating form, and the particular kinds of form affected by the artists of one generation, have an important bearing on the art of the next. For whereas the methods and forms of one may admit of almost infinite development, the methods and forms of another may admit of nothing but imitation. For instance, the fifteenth century movement that began with Masaccio, Uccello, and Castagno opened up a rich vein of rather inferior ore; whereas the school of Raffael was a blind alley. Cézanne discovered methods and forms which have revealed a vista of possibilities to the end of which no man can see; on the instrument that he invented thousands of artists yet unborn may play their own tunes.

What the future will owe to Cézanne we cannot guess: what contemporary art owes to him it would be hard to compute. Without him the artists of genius and talent who to-day delight us with the significance and originality of their work might have remained port-bound for ever, ill-discerning their objective, wanting chart, rudder, and compass. Cézanne is the Christopher Columbus of a new continent of form. In 1839 he was born at Aix-en-Provence, and for forty years he painted patiently in the manner of his master Pissarro. To the eyes of the world he appeared, so far as he appeared at all, a respectable, minor Impressionist, an admirer of Manet, a friend, if not a protégé, of Zola, a loyal, negligible disciple. He was on the right side, of course—the Impressionist side, the side of the honest, disinterested artists, against the academic, literary pests. He believed in painting. He believed that it could be something better than an expensive substitute for photography or an accompaniment to poor poetry. So in 1870 he was for science against sentimentality.

But science will neither make nor satisfy an artist: and perhaps Cézanne saw what the great Impressionists could not see, that though they were still painting exquisite pictures their theories had led art into a *cul de sac*. So while he was working away in his corner of Provence, shut off completely from the aestheticism of Paris, from Baudelairism and Whistlerism, Cézanne was always looking for something to replace the bad science of Claude Monet. And somewhere about 1880 he found it. At Aix-en-Provence came to him a revelation that has set a gulf between the nineteenth century and the twentieth: for, gazing at the familiar landscape, Cézanne came to understand it, not as a mode of light, nor yet as a player in the game of human life, but as an end in itself and an object of intense emotion. Every great artist has seen landscape as an end in itself—as pure form, that is to say; Cézanne had made a generation of artists feel that compared with its significance as an end in itself all else about a landscape is negligible. From that time forward Cézanne set himself to create forms that would express the emotion that he felt for what he had learnt to see. Science became as irrelevant as subject. Everything can be seen as pure form, and behind pure form lurks the mysterious significance that thrills to ecstasy. The rest of Cézanne's life is a continuous effort to capture and express the significance of form.

I have tried to say in another place that there are more roads than one by which a man may come at reality. Some artists seem to have come at it by sheer force of imagination, unaided by anything without them; they have needed no material ladder to help them out of matter. They have spoken with reality as mind to mind, and have passed on the message in forms which owe nothing but bare existence to the physical universe. Of this race are the best musicians and architects; of this race is not Cézanne. He travelled towards reality along the traditional road of European painting. It was in what he saw that he discovered a sublime architecture haunted by that Universal which informs every Particular. He pushed further and further towards a complete revelation of the significance of form, but he needed something concrete as a point of departure. It was because Cézanne could come at reality only through what he saw that he never invented purely abstract forms. Few great artists have depended more on the model. Every picture carried him a little further towards his goal— complete expression; and because it was not the making of pictures but the expression of his sense of the significance of form that he cared about, he lost interest in his work so soon as he had made it express as much as he had grasped. His own pictures were for Cézanne nothing but rungs in a ladder at the top of which would be complete expression. The whole of his later life was a climbing towards an ideal. For him every picture was a means, a step, a stick, a hold, a stepping-stone—something he was ready to discard as soon as it had served his purpose. He had no use for his own pictures. To him they were experiments. He tossed them into bushes, or left them in the open fields to be stumbling-blocks for a future race of luckless critics.

Cézanne is a type of the perfect artist; he is the perfect antithesis of the professional picture-maker, or poem-maker, or music-maker. He created forms because only by so doing could he accomplish the end of his existence —the expression of his sense of the significance of form. When we are talking about aesthetics, very properly we brush all this aside, and consider only the object and its emotional effect on us; but when we are trying to explain the emotional effectiveness of pictures we turn naturally to the minds of the men who made them, and find in the

story of Cézanne an inexhaustible spring of suggestion. His
life was a constant effort to create forms that would express what he felt in the moment of inspiration. The notion
of uninspired art, of a formula for making pictures, would
have appeared to him preposterous. The real business of
his life was not to make pictures, but to work out his
own salvation. Fortunately for us he could only do this
by painting. Any two pictures by Cézanne are bound to
differ profoundly. He never dreamed of repeating himself.
He could not stand still. That is why a whole generation
of otherwise dissimilar artists have drawn inspiration from
his work. That is why it implies no disparagement of any
living artist when I say that the prime characteristic of
the new movement is its derivation from Cézanne.

The world into which Cézanne tumbled was a world
still agitated by the quarrels of Romantics and Realists. The
quarrel between Romance and Realism is the quarrel of
people who cannot agree as to whether the history of Spain
or the number of pips is the more important thing about
an orange. The Romantics and Realists were deaf men
coming to blows about the squeak of a bat. The instinct
of a Romantic invited to say what he felt about anything
was to recall its associations. A rose, for instance, made
him think of old gardens and young ladies and Edmund
Waller and sundials, and a thousand quaint and gracious
things that, at one time or another, had befallen him or
someone else. A rose touched life at a hundred pretty
points. A rose was interesting because it had a past. "Bosh,"
said the Realist, "I will tell you what a rose is; that is to
say, I will give you a detailed account of the properties
of *Rosa setigera*, not forgetting to mention the urn-shaped
calyx-tube, the five imbricated lobes, or the open corolla
of five obovate petals." To a Cézanne one account would
appear as irrelevant as the other, since both omit the thing
that matters—what philosophers used to call "the thing in
itself," what now, I imagine, they call "the essential reality."
For, after all, what is a rose? What is a tree, a dog, a wall,
a boat? What is the particular significance of anything?
Certainly the essence of a boat is not that it conjures up

visions of argosies with purple sails, nor yet that it carries coals to Newcastle. Imagine a boat in complete isolation, detach it from man and his urgent activities and fabulous history, what is it that remains, what is that to which we still react emotionally? What but pure form, and that which, lying behind pure form, gives it its significance. It was for this Cézanne felt the emotion he spent his life in expressing. And the second characteristic of the new movement is a passionate interest, inherited from Cézanne, in things regarded as ends in themselves. In saying this I am saying no more than that the painters of the movement are consciously determined to be artists. Peculiarity lies in the consciousness—the consciousness with which they set themselves to eliminate all that lies between themselves and the pure forms of things. To be an artist, they think, suffices. How many men of talent, and even of genius, have missed being effective artists because they tried to be something else?

2. SIMPLIFICATION AND DESIGN

AT THE risk of becoming a bore I repeat that there is
something ludicrous about hunting for characteristics
in the art of to-day or of yesterday, or of any particular
period. In art the only important distinction is the distinction between good art and bad. That this pot was made in
Mesopotamia about 4000 B.C., and that picture in Paris
about 1913 A.D., is of very little consequence. Nevertheless,
it is possible, though not very profitable, to distinguish
between equally good works made at different times in
different places; and although the practice of associating
art with the age in which it was produced can be of no
service to art or artists, I am not sure that it can be of
no service whatever. For if it be true that art is an index
to the spiritual condition of an age, the historical consideration of art cannot fail to throw some light on the
history of civilisation. It is conceivable therefore that a
comparative study of artistic periods might lead us to
modify our conception of human development, and to
revise a few of our social and political theories. Be that
as it may, this much is sure: should anyone wish to infer
from the art it produced the civility of an age, he must be
capable of distinguishing the work of that age from the
work of all other ages. He must be familiar with the
characteristics of the movement. It is my intention to indicate a few of the more obvious characteristics of the
contemporary movement.

But how comes it that the art of one age differs from
that of another? At first sight it seems odd that art, which
is the expression of man's sense of the significance of
form, should vary even superficially from age to age. Yet,
deeply considered, it is as certain that superficially art will
always be changing as that essentially it cannot change. It

seems that the ape-instinct in man is so strong ~~that unless he were continually changing he would cease to create and merely imitate~~. It is the old question of the artistic problem. Only by setting himself new problems can the artist raise his powers to the white heat of creation. The forms in which artists can express themselves are infinite, and their desire to express themselves keeps up a constant change and reaction in artistic form. Not only is there something of the ancestral ape in man, there is something of the ancestral sheep; there are fashions in forms and colours and the relations of forms and colours; or, to put the matter more pleasantly, and more justly, there is sufficient accord in the sensibilities of an age to induce a certain similarity of forms. It seems as though there were strange powers in the air from which no man can altogether escape; we call them by ~~pet names~~—"Movements," "Forces," "Tendencies," "Influences," "The Spirit of the Age"—but we never understand them. They are neither to be frightened nor cajoled by our airs of familiarity, which impress the public only. They exist, however, and if they did not we should have to invent them; for how else are we to explain the fact that not only do the artists of a particular period affect particular kinds of form, but that even the spectators of each new generation seem to be born with sensibilities specially apt to be flattered by them. In this age it is possible to take refuge under the magic word "Cézanne"; ~~we can say that Cézanne has imposed his forms on Georgian painters and public, just as Wagner imposed his on Edwardian musicians and concertgoers~~. This explanation seems to me inadequate; and in any case it will not account for the predominance of formal fashions in ages undominated by any masterful genius. ~~The spirit of an artistic age is, I suspect, a composition that defies complete analysis; the work of one great mind is generally one part of it, the monuments of some particular past age are often another.~~ Technical discoveries have sometimes led to artistic changes. For instance, to men who have been in the habit of painting on wood, the invention of canvas would suggest all sorts of fascinating novelties. Lastly, there is a continual change in the appearance of those familiar objects which are the raw material of most visual artists. So, though the essential quality —significance—is constant, in the choice of forms there is perpetual change; and these changes seem to move in long flights or shorter jumps, so that we are able, with some precision, to lay our fingers on two points between which there is a certain amount of art possessing certain common characteristics. That which lies between two such points historians call a period or movement.

The period in which we find ourselves in the year 1913 begins with the maturity of Cézanne (about 1885). It therefore overlaps the Impressionist movement, which certainly had life in it till the end of the nineteenth century. Whether Post-Impressionism will peter out as Impressionism has done, or whether it is the first flowering of a new artistic vitality with centuries of development before it, is, I have admitted, a matter of conjecture. What seems to me certain is that those who shall be able to contemplate our age as something complete, as a period in the history of art, will not so much as know of the existence of the artisans still amongst us who create illusions and chaffer and quarrel in the tradition of the Victorians. When they think of the early twentieth-century painters they will think only of the artists who tried to create form—the artisans who tried to create illusions will be forgotten. They will think of the men who looked to the present, not of those who looked to the past; and, therefore, it is of them alone that I shall think when I attempt to describe the contemporary movement.[1]

Already I have suggested two characteristics of the movement; I have said that in their choice of forms and colours

[1] Of course there are some good artists alive who owe nothing to Cézanne. Fortunately two of Cézanne's contemporaries, Degas and Renoir, are still at work. Also there are a few who belong to the older movement, *e.g.* Mr. Walter Sickert, M. Simon Bussy, M. Vuillard, Mr. J. W. Morrice. I should be as unwilling to omit these names from a history of twentieth century art as to include them in a chapter devoted to the contemporary movement.

most vital contemporary artists are, more or less, influenced by Cézanne, and that Cézanne has inspired them with the resolution to free their art from literary and scientific irrelevancies. Most people, asked to mention a third, would promptly answer, I suspect—Simplification. To instance simplification as a peculiarity of the art of any particular age seems queer, since simplification is essential to all art. Without it art cannot exist; for art is the creation of significant form, and simplification is the liberating of what is significant from what is not. Yet to such depths had art sunk in the nineteenth century, that in the eyes of the rabble the greatest crime of Whistler and the Impressionists was their by no means drastic simplification. And we are not yet clear of the Victorian slough. The spent dip stinks on into the dawn. You have only to look at almost any modern building to see masses of elaboration and detail that form no part of any real design and serve no useful purpose. Nothing stands in greater need of simplification than architecture, and nowhere is simplification more dreaded and detested than amongst architects. Walk the streets of London; everywhere you will see huge blocks of ready-made decoration, pilasters and porticoes, friezes and façades, hoisted on cranes to hang from ferro-concrete walls. Public buildings have become public laughing-stocks. They are as senseless as slag-heaps, and far less beautiful. Only where economy has banished the architect do we see masonry of any merit. The engineers, who have at least a scientific problem to solve, create, in factories and railway-bridges, our most creditable monuments. They at least are not ashamed of their construction, or, at any rate, they are not allowed to smother it in beauty at thirty shillings a foot. We shall have no more architecture in Europe till architects understand that all these tawdry excrescences have got to be simplified away, till they make up their minds to express themselves in the materials of the age—steel concrete, and glass—and to create in these admirable media vast, simple, and significant forms.

The contemporary movement has pushed simplification a great deal further than Manet and his friends pushed it, thereby distinguishing itself from anything we have seen since the twelfth century. Since the twelfth century, in sculpture and glass, the thirteenth, in painting and drawing, the drift has been towards realism and away from art. Now the essence of realism is detail. Since Zola, every novelist has known that nothing gives so imposing an air of reality as a mass of irrelevant facts, and very few have cared to give much else. Detail is the heart of realism, and the fatty degeneration of art. The tendency of the movement is to simplify away all this mess of detail which painters have introduced into pictures in order to state facts. But more than this was needed. There were irrelevancies introduced into pictures for other purposes than that of statement. There were the irrelevancies of technical swagger. Since the twelfth century there has been a steady elaboration of technical complexities. Writers with nothing to say soon come to regard the manipulation of words as an end in itself. So cooks without eggs might come to regard the ritual of omelette-making, the mixing of condiments, the chopping of herbs, the stoking of fires, and the shaping of white caps, as a fine art. As for the eggs—why, that's God's business: and who wants omelettes when he can have cooking? The movement has simplified the *batterie de cuisine*. Nothing is to be left in a work of art which merely shows that the craftsman knows how to put it there.

Alas! It generally turns out that Life and Art are rather more complicated than we could wish; to understand exactly what is meant by simplification we must go deeper into the mysteries. It is easy to say eliminate irrelevant details. What details are not irrelevant? In a work of art nothing is relevant but what contributes to formal significance. Therefore all informatory matter is irrelevant and should be eliminated. But what most painters have to express can only be expressed in designs so complex and subtle that without some clue they would be almost unintelligible. For instance, there are many designs that can only be grasped by a spectator who looks at them from a particular point of view. Not every picture is as good seen upside down as upside up. To be sure, very sensitive people can always discover from the design itself how it should be viewed, and, without much difficulty, will place correctly a piece of lace or embroidery in which there is no informatory clue to guide them. Nevertheless, when an artist makes an intricate design it is tempting and, indeed, reasonable, for him to wish to provide a clue; and to do so he has only to work into his design some familiar object, a tree or a figure, and the business is done. Having established a number of extremely subtle relations between highly complex forms, he may ask himself whether anyone else will be able to appreciate them. Shall he not give a hint as to the nature of his organisation, and ease the way for our aesthetic emotions? If he give to his forms so much of the appearance of the forms of ordinary life that we shall at once refer them back to something we have already seen, shall we not grasp more easily their aesthetic relations in his design? Enter by the back-door representation in the quality of a clue to the nature of design. I have no objection to its presence. Only, if the representative element is not to ruin the picture as a work of art, it must be fused into the design. It must do double duty; as well as giving information, it must create aesthetic emotion. It must be simplified into significant form.

Let us make no mistake about this. To help the spectator to appreciate our design we have introduced into our picture a representative or cognitive element. This element has nothing whatever to do with art. The recognition of a correspondence between the forms of a work of art and the familiar forms of life cannot possibly provoke aesthetic emotion. Only significant form can do that. Of course realistic forms may be aesthetically significant, and out of them an artist may create a superb work of art, but it is with their aesthetic and not with their cognitive value that we shall then be concerned. We shall treat them as though they were not representative of anything. The cognitive or representative element in a work of art can be useful as a means to the perception of formal relations and in no other way. It is valuable to the spectator, but it is of no value to the work of art; or rather it is valuable to the work of art as an ear-trumpet is valuable to one who would converse with the deaf: the speaker could do as well without it, the listener could not. The representative element may help the spectator; it can do the picture no good and it may do harm. It may ruin the design; that is to say, it may deprive the picture of its value as a whole; and it is as a whole, as an organisation of forms, that a work of art provokes the most tremendous emotions.

From the point of view of the spectator the Post-Impressionists have been particularly happy in their simplification. As we know, a design can be composed just as well of realistic forms as of invented; but a fine design composed of realistic forms runs a great risk of being aesthetically underrated. We are so immediately struck by the representative element that the formal significance passes us by. It is very hard at first sight to appreciate the design of a picture by a highly realistic artist—Ingres, for instance; our aesthetic emotions are overlaid by our human curiosity. We do not see the figures as forms, because we immediately think of them as people. On the other hand, a design composed of purely imaginery forms, without any cognitive clue (say a Persia carpet), if it be at all elaborate and intricate, is apt to non-plus the less sensitive spectators. Post-Impressionists, by employing forms sufficiently distorted to disconcert and baffle human interest and curiosity yet sufficiently representative to call immediate attention to the nature of the design, have found a short way to our aesthetic emotions. This does not make Post-Impressionist pictures better or worse than others; it makes them more easily appreciable as works of art. Probably it will always be difficult for the mass of men to consider pictures as works of art, but it will be less difficult for them so to consider Post-Impressionist than realistic pictures; while, if they ceased to consider objects unprovided with representative clues (*e.g.* some oriental textiles) as historical monuments, they would find it very difficult to consider them at all.

To assure his design, the artist makes it his first care to

simplify. But mere simplification, the elimination of detail, is not enough. The informatory forms that remain have got to be made significant. The representative element, if it is not to injure the design, must become a part of it; besides giving information it has got to provoke aesthetic emotion. That is where symbolism fails. The symbolist eliminates, but does not assimilate. His symbols, as a rule, are not significant forms, but formal intelligencers. They are not integral parts of a plastic conception, but intellectual abbreviations. They are not informed by the artist's emotion, they are invented by his intellect. They are dead matter in a living organism. They are rigid and tight because they are not traversed by the rhythm of the design. The explanatory legends that illustrators used to produce from the mouths of their characters are not more foreign to visual art than the symbolic forms with which many able draughts men have ruined their designs. In the famous "Melancholia," and, to some extent, in a few other engravings—"St. Eustace," for instance, and "The Virgin and Child" (B. 34. British Museum),—Dürer has managed to convert a mass of detail into tolerably significant form; but in the greater part of his work (e.g. "The Knight," "St. Jerome") fine conception is hopelessly ruined by a mass of undigested symbolism.

Every form in a work of art has, then, to be made aesthetically significant; also every form has to be made a part of a significant whole. For, as generally happens, the value of the parts combined into a whole is far greater than the value of the sum of the parts. This organisation of forms into a significant whole is called Design; and an insistence—an exaggerated insistence some will say—on design is the fourth characteristic of the Contemporary Movement. This insistence, this conviction that a work should not be good on the whole, but as a whole, is, no doubt, in part a reaction from the rather too easy virtue of some of the Impressionists, who were content to cover their canvases with charming forms and colours, not caring overmuch whether or how they were co-ordinated. Certainly this was a weakness in Impressionism—though by no means in all the Impressionist masters—for it is certain that the profoundest emotions are provoked by significant combinations of significant forms. Also, it seems certain that only in these organised combinations can the artist express himself completely.

It seems that an artist creates a good design when, having been possessed by a real emotional conception, he is able to hold and translate it. We all agree, I think, that till the artist has had his moment of emotional vision there can be no very considerable work of art; but, the vision seen and felt, it still remains uncertain whether he has the force to hold and the skill to translate it. Of course the vast majority of pictures fail in design because they correspond to no emotional vision; but the interesting failures are those in which the vision came but was incompletely grasped. Tht painters who have failed for want of technical skill to set down what they have felt and mastered could be counted on the fingers of one hand—if, indeed, there are any to be counted. But on all sides we see interesting pictures in which the holes in the artist's conception are obvious. The vision was once perfect, but it cannot be recaptured. The rapture will not return. The supreme creative power is wanting. There are holes, and they have to be filled with putty. Putty we all know when we see it— when we feel it. It is dead matter—literal transcriptions from nature, intellectual machinery, forms that correspond with nothing that was apprehended emotionally, forms unfired with the rhythm that thrilled through the first vision of a significant whole.

There is an absolute necessity about a good design arising, I imagine, from the fact that the nature of each form and its relation to all the other forms is determined by the artist's need of expressing exactly what he felt. Of course, a perfect correspondence between expression and conception may not be established at the first or the second attempt. But if the work is to be a success there will come a moment in which the artist will be able to hold and express completely his hour or minute of inspiration. If that moment does not come the design will lack

necessity. For though an artist's aesthetic sense enables
him, as we shall see, to say whether a design is right or
wrong, only this masterful power of seizing and holding
his vision enables him to make it right. A bad design lacks
cohesion; a good design possesses it; if I conjecture that
the secret of cohesion is the complete realisation of that
thrill which comes to an artist when he conceives his work
as a whole, I shall not forget that it is a conjecture. But it
is not conjecture to say that when we call a design good
we mean that, as a whole, it provokes aesthetic emotion,
and that a bad design is a congeries of lines and colours,
individually satisfactory perhaps, but as a whole unmoving.

For, ultimately, the spectator can determine whether a
design is good or bad only by discovering whether or no
it moves him. Having made that discovery he can go on
to criticise in detail; but the beginning of all aesthetic judgment and all criticism is emotion. It is after I have been
left cold that I begin to notice that defective organisation
of forms which I call bad design. And here, in my judgments about particular designs, I am still on pretty sure
ground: it is only when I attempt to account for the moving
power of certain combinations that I get into the world of
conjecture. Nevertheless, I believe that mine are no bad
guesses at truth, and that on the same hypothesis we can
account for the difference between good and bad drawing.

Design is the organisation of forms: drawing is the
shaping of the forms themselves. Clearly there is a point at
which the two commingle, but that is a matter of no
present importance. When I say that drawing is bad, I
mean that I am not moved by the contours of the forms
that make up the work of art. The causes of bad drawing
and bad design I believe to be similar. A form is badly
drawn when it does not correspond with a part of an
emotional conception. The shape of every form in a work
of art should be imposed on the artist by his inspiration.
The hand of the artist, I believe, must be guided by the
necessity of expressing something he has felt not only
intensely but definitely. The artist must know what he is
about, and what he is about must be, if I am right, the

translation into material form of something that he felt in a spasm of ecstasy. Therefore, shapes that merely fill gaps will be ill-drawn. Forms that are not dictated by any emotional necessity, forms that state facts, forms that are the consequences of a theory of draughtsmanship, imitations of natural objects or of the forms of other works of art, forms that exist merely to fill spaces—padding in fact, —all these are worthless. Good drawing must be inspired, it must be the natural manifestation of that thrill which accompanies the passionate apprehension of form.

One word more to close this discussion. No critic is so stupid as to mean by "bad drawing," drawing that does not represent the model correctly. The gods of the art schools, Michelangelo, Mantegna, Raffael, &c. played the oddest tricks with anatomy. Everyone knows that Giotto's figures are less accurately drawn than those of Sir Edward Poynter; no one supposes that they are not drawn better. We do possess a criterion by which we can judge drawing, and that criterion can have nothing to do with truth to nature. We judge drawing by concentrating our aesthetic sensibility on a particular part of design. What we mean when we speak of "good drawing" and "bad drawing" is not doubtful; we mean "aesthetically moving" and "aesthetically insignificant." Why some drawing moves and some does not is a very different question. I have put forward an hypothesis of which I could write a pretty sharp criticism: that task, however, I leave to more willing hands. Only this I will say: just as a competent musician knows with certainty when an instrument is out of tune though the criterion resides nowhere but in his own sensibility; so a fine critic of visual art can detect lines and colours that are not alive. Whether he be looking at an embroidered pattern or at a careful anatomical study, the task is always the same, because the criterion is always the same. What he has to decide is whether the drawing is, or is not, aesthetically significant.

Insistence on design is perhaps the most obvious characteristic of the movement. To all are familiar those circumambient black lines that are intended to give definition

to forms and to reveal the construction of the picture.
For almost all the younger artists—Bonnard is an obvious
exception—affect that architectural method of design which
indeed has generally been preferred by European artists.
The difference between "architectural design" and what I
call "imposed design" will be obvious to anyone who com-
pares a picture by Cézanne with a picture by Whistler.
Better still, compare any first-rate Florentine of the fourteenth or fifteenth century with any Sung picture. Here are
two methods of achieving the same end, equally good, so
far as I can judge, and as different as possible. We feel
towards a picture by Cézanne or Masaccio or Giotto as we
feel towards a Romanesque church; the design seems to
spring upwards, mass piles itself on mass, forms balance
each other masonrywise: there is a sense of strain, and
of strength to meet it. Turn to a Chinese picture; the forms
seem to be pinned to the silk or to be hung from above.
There is no sense of thrust or strain; rather there is the
felling of some creeper, with roots we know not where,
that hangs itself in exquisite festoons along the wall.
Though architectural design is a permanent characteristic
of Western art, of four periods I think it would be fairly
accurate to say that it is a characteristic so dominant as
to be distinctive; and they are Byzantine VIth Century,
Byzantine IX-XIIIth Century, Florentine XIVth and XVth
Century, and the Contemporary Movement.

To say that the artists of the movement insist on design
is not to deny that some of them are exceptionally fine
colourists. Cézanne is one of the greatest colourists that
ever lived; Henri-Matisse is a great colourist. Yet all, or
nearly all, use colour as a mode of form. They design in
colour, that is in coloured shapes. Very few fall into the
error of regarding colour as an end in itself, and of trying
to think of it as something different from form. Colour
in itself has little or no significance. The mere juxtaposition
of tones moves us hardly at all. As colourists themselves
are fond of saying, "It is the quantities that count." It is
not by his mixing and choosing, but by the shapes of
his colours, and the combinations of those shapes, that

we recognise the colourist. Colour becomes significant only when it becomes form. It is a virtue in contemporary artists that they have set their faces against the practice of juxtaposing pretty patches of colour without much considering their formal relations, and that they attempt so to organise tones as to raise form to its highest significance. But it is not surprising that a generation of exceptionally sweet and attractive but rather formless colourists should be shocked by the obtrusion of those black lines that seem to do violence to their darling. They are irritated by pictures in which there is to be no accidental charm of soft lapses and lucky chiaroscuro. They do not admire the austere determination of these young men to make their work independent and self-supporting and unbeholden to adventitious dainties. They cannot understand this passion for works that are admirable as wholes, this fierce insistence on design, this willingness to leave bare the construction if by so doing the spectator may be helped to a conception of the plan. Critics of the Impressionist age are vexed by the naked bones and muscles of Post-Impressionist pictures. But, for my own part, even though these young artists insisted on a bareness and baldness exceeding anything we have yet seen, I should be far from blaming a band of ascetics who in an age of unorganised prettiness insisted on the paramount importance of design.

coln alone evokes emotion

3. THE PATHETIC FALLACY

MANY of those who are enthusiastic about the movement, were they asked what they considered its most important characteristic, would reply, I imagine, "The expression of a new and peculiar point of view." "Post-Impressionism," I have heard people say, "is an expression of the ideas and feelings of that spiritual renaissance which is now growing into a lusty revolution." With this I cannot, of course, agree. If art expresses anything, it expresses some profound and general emotion common, or at least possible, to all ages, and peculiar to none. But if these sympathetic people mean, as I believe they do, that the art of the new movement is a manifestation of something different from—they will say larger than—itself, of a spiritual revolution in fact, I will not oppose them. Art is as good an index to the spiritual state of this age as of another; and in the effort of artists to free painting from the clinging conventions of the near past, and to use it as a means only to the most sublime emotions, we may read signs of an age possessed of a new sense of values and eager to turn that possession to account. It is impossible to visit a good modern exhibition without feeling that we are back in a world not altogether unworthy to be compared with that which produced primitive art. Here are men who take art seriously. Perhaps they take life seriously too, but if so, that is only because there are things in life (aesthetic ecstasy, for instance) worth taking seriously. In life, they can distinguish between the wood and the few fine trees. As for art, they know that it is something more important than a criticism of life; they will not pretend that it is a traffic in amenities; they know that it is a spiritual necessity. They are not making handsome furniture, nor pretty knick-

knacks, nor tasteful souvenirs; they are creating forms that
stir our most wonderful emotions.

It is tempting to suppose that art such as this implies an
attitude towards society. It seems to imply a belief that the
future will not be a mere repetition of the past, but that
by dint of willing and acting men will conquer for themselves a life in which the claims of spirit and emotion will
make some headway against the necessities of physical
existence. It seems, I say: but it would be exceedingly rash
to assume anything of the sort, and, for myself, I doubt
whether the good artist bothers much more about the future
than about the past. Why should artists bother about the
fate of humanity? If art does not justify itself, aesthetic
rapture does. Whether that rapture is to be felt by future
generations of virtuous and contented artisans is a matter
of purely speculative interest. Rapture suffices. The artist
has no more call to look forward than the lover in the arms
of his mistress. There are moments in life that are ends to
which the whole history of humanity would not be an
extravagant means; of such are the moments of aesthetic
ecstasy. It is as vain to imagine that the artist works with
one eye on The Great State of the future, as to go to his
art for an expression of political or social opinions. It is
not their attitude towards the State or towards life, but the
pure and serious attitude of these artists towards their art,
that makes the movement significant of the age. Here are
men who refuse all compromise, who will hire no half-way
house between what they believe and what the public likes;
men who decline flatly, and over-stridently sometimes, to
concern themselves at all with what seems to them unimportant. To call the art of the movement democratic—
some people have done so—is silly. All artists are aristo-
crats in a sense, since no artist believes honestly in human
equality; in any other sense to call an artist an aristocrat
or a democrat is to call him something irrelevant or
insulting. The man who creates art especially to move the
poor, or especially to please the rich, prostitutes whatever
of worth may be in him. A good many artists have maimed
or ruined themselves by pretending that, besides the distinc-

tion between good art and bad, there is a distinction between aristocratic art and plebeian. In a sense all art is
anarchical; to take art seriously is to be unable to take
seriously the conventions and principles by which societies
exist. It may be said with some justice that Post-Impressionism is peculiarly anarchical because it insists so em-
phatically on fundamentals and challenges so violently the
conventional tradition of art and, by implication, I suppose,
the conventional view of life. By setting art so high, it sets
industrial civilisation very low. Here, then, it may shake
hands with the broader and vaguer spirit of the age; the
effort to produce serious art may bear witness to a stir in
the underworld, to a weariness of smug materialism and a
more passionate and spiritual conception of life. The art
of the movement, in so far as it is art, expresses nothing
temporal or local; but it may be a manifestation of something that is happening here and now, something of which
the majority of mankind seems hardly yet to be aware.

Men and women who have been thrilled by the pure
aesthetic significance of a work of art go away into the
outer world in a state of excitement and exaltation which
makes them more sensitive to all that is going forward
about them. Thus, they realise with a heightened intensity
the significance and possibility of life. It is not surprising
that they should read this new sense of life into that which
gave it. Not in the least; and I shall not quarrel with them
for doing so. It is far more important to be moved by art
than to know precisely what it is that moves. I should just
like to remind them, though, that if art were no more than
they sometimes fancy it to be, art would not move them
as it does. If art were a mere matter of suggesting the
emotions of life a work of art would give to each no more
than what each brought with him. It is because art adds
something new to our emotional experience, something that
comes not from human life but from pure form, that it stirs
us so deeply and so mysteriously. But that, for many, art
not only adds something new, but seems to transmute and
enrich the old, is certain and by no means deplorable.

The fact is, this passionate and austere art of the Con-

temporary Movement is not only an index to the general
ferment, it is also the inspiration, and even the standard,
of a young, violent, and fierce generation. It is the most
visible and the most successful manifestation of their will,
or they think it is. Political reform, social reform, literature
even, move slowly, ankle-deep in the mud of materialism
and deliquescent tradition. Though not without reason
Socialists claim that Liberals ride their horses, the jockeys
still wear blue and buff. Mr. Lloyd George stands un-
steadily on the shoulders of Mr. Gladstone; the bulk of his
colleagues cling on behind. If literature is to be made the
test, we shall soon be wishing ourselves back in the nineteenth century. Unless it be Thomas Hardy, there is no
first-rate novelist in Europe; there is no first-rate poet;
without disrespect to D'Annunzio, Shaw, or Claudel, it may
be said that Ibsen was their better. Since Mozart, music has
just kept her nose above the slough of realism, romance,
and melodrama. Music seems to be where painting was in
the time of Courbet; she is drifting through complex intellectualism and a brilliant, exasperating realism, to arrive,
I hope, at greater purity.[1] Contemporary painting is the one
manifest triumph of the young age. Not even the oldest
and wisest dare try to smile it away. Those who cannot
love Cézanne and Matisse hate them; and they not only
say it, they shriek it. It is not surprising, then, that visual
art, which seems to many the mirror in which they see
realised their own ideals, should have become for some a
new religion. Not content with its aesthetic significance,
these seek in art an inspiration for the whole of life. For
some of us, to be sure, the aesthetic significance is a sufficient inspiration; for the others I have no hard words.
To art they take their most profound and subtle emotions,
their most magnanimous ideas, their dearest hopes; from
art they bring away enriched and purified emotion and
exaltation, and fresh sources of both. In art they imagine

[1] June 1913. *Ariadne auf Naxos.* Is Strauss, our one musician
of genius, himself the pivot on which the wheel is beginning
to swing? Having drained the cup of Wagnerism and turned
it upside down, is he now going to school with Mozart?

that they find an expression of their most intimate and mysterious feelings; and, though they miss, not utterly but to some extent, the best that art has to give, if of art they make a religion I do not blame them.

In the days of Alexander Severus there lived at Rome a Greek freed man. As he was a clever craftsman his lot was not hard. His body was secure, his belly full, his hands and brain pleasantly busy. He lived amongst intelligent people and handsome objects, permitting himself such reasonable emotions as were recommended by his master, Epicurus. He awoke each morning to a quiet day of ordered satisfaction, the prescribed toll of unexacting labour, a little sensual pleasure, a little rational conversation, a cool argument, a judicious appreciation of all that the intellect can apprehend. Into this existence burst suddenly a cranky fanatic, with a religion. To the Greek it seemed that the breath of life had blown through the grave, imperial streets. Yet nothing in Rome was changed, save one immortal, or mortal, soul. The same waking eyes opened on the same objects; yet all was changed; all was charged with meaning. New things existed. Everything mattered. In the vast equality of religious emotion the Greek forgot his status and his nationality. His life became a miracle and an ecstasy. As a lover awakes, he awoke to a day full of consequence and delight. He had learnt to feel; and, because to feel a man must live, it was good to be alive. I know an erudite and intelligent man, a man whose arid life had been little better than one long cold in the head, for whom that madman, Van Gogh, did nothing less.

V

THE FUTURE

---

1. SOCIETY AND ART

TO BOTHER much about anything but the present is, we all agree, beneath the dignity of a healthy human animal. Yet how many of us can resist the malsane pleasure of puzzling over the past and speculating about the future? Once admit that the Contemporary Movement is something a little out of the common, that it has the air of a beginning, and you will catch yourself saying "Beginning of what?" instead of settling down quietly to enjoy the rare spectacle of a renaissance. Art, we hope, serious, alive, and independent is knocking at the door, and we are impelled to ask "What will come of it?" This is the general question, which, you will find, divides itself into two sufficiently precise queries—"What will Society do with Art?" and "What will Art do with Society?"

It is a mistake to suppose that because Society cannot affect Art directly, it cannot affect it at all. Society can affect Art indirectly because it can affect artists directly. Clearly, if the creation of works of art were made a capital offence, the quantity, if not the quality, of artistic output would be affected. Proposals less barbarous, but far more terrible, are from time to time put forward by cultivated state-projectors who would make of artists, not criminals, but highly-paid officials. Though statesmanship can do no positive good to art, it can avoid doing a great deal of harm: its power for ill is considerable. The one good thing Society can do for the artist is to leave him alone. Give him liberty. The more completely the artist is freed from the pressure of public taste and opinion, from the hope of rewards and the menace of morals, from the fear of absolute starvation or punishment, and from the prospect of wealth or popular consideration, the better for him and the better for art, and therefore the better for everyone.

Liberate the artist: here is something that those powerful
and important people who are always assuring us that they
would do anything for art can do.

They might begin the work of encouragement by dis-
establishing and disendowing art; by withdrawing doles
from art schools, and confiscating the moneys misused by
the Royal Academy. The case of the schools is urgent. Art
schools do nothing but harm, because they must do something. Art is not to be learned; at any rate it is not to be
taught. All that the drawing-master can teach is the craft
of imitation. In schools there must be a criterion of excellence and that criterion cannot be an artistic one; the
drawing-master sets up the only criterion he is capable of
using—fidelity to the model. No master can make a student
into an artist; but all can, and most do, turn into impostors,
maniacs, criminals, or just cretins, the unfortunate boys and
girls who had been made artists by nature. It is not the
master's fault and he ought not to be blamed. He is there
to bring all his pupils to a certain standard of efficiency
appreciable by inspectors and by the general public, and
the only quality of which such can judge is verisimilitude.
The only respects in which one work can be seen to differ
from another by an ordinarily insensitive person (*e.g.* a
Board of Education inspector) are choice of subject and
fidelity to common vision. So, even if a drawing-master
could recognise artistic talent, he would not be permitted
to encourage it. It is not that drawing-masters are wicked,
but that the system is vicious. Art schools must go.

The money that the State at present devotes to the dis-
couragement of Art had better, I dare say, be given to the
rich. It would be tempting to save it for the purchase of
works of art, but perhaps that can lead to nothing but mischief. It is unthinkable that any Government should ever
buy what is best in the work of its own age; it is a question
how far purchase by the State even of fine old pictures is
a benefit to art. It is not a question that need be discussed;
for though a State may have amongst its employés men
who can recognise a fine work of art, provided it be
sufficiently old, a modern State will be careful to thwart

and stultify their dangerously good taste. State-acquisition
of fine ancient art might or might not be a means to good
—I daresay it would be; but the purchase of third-rate old
masters and *objets d'art* can benefit no one except the
dealers. As I shall hope to show, something might be said
for supporting and enriching galleries and museums, if only
the public attitude towards, and the official conception of,
these places could be changed. As for contemporary art,
official patronage is the surest method of encouraging in it
all that is most stupid and pernicious. Our public monuments, the statues and buildings that disgrace our streets,
our postage-stamps, coins, and official portraits are mere
bait to the worst instincts of the worst art-students and
to the better a formidable temptation.

Some of those generous prophets who sit at home dream-
ing of pure communistic societies have been good enough
to find a place in them for the artist. Demos is to keep
for his diversion a kennel of mountebanks. Artists will be
chosen by the State and supported by the State. The people
will pay the piper and call the tune. In the choice of
politicians the method works well enough, but to art it
would be fatal. The creation of soft artistic jobs is the
most unlikely method of encouraging art. Already hundreds take to it, not because they have in them that which
must be expressed, but because art seems to offer a
pleasant and genteel career. When the income is assured
the number of those who fancy art as a profession will
not diminish. On the contrary, in the great State of the
future the competition will be appalling I can imagine
the squeezing and intriguing between the friends of ap-
plicants and their parliamentary deputies, between the
deputies and the Minister of Fine Arts; and I can imagine
the art produced to fulfil a popular mandate in the days
when private jobbery will be the only check on public
taste. Can we not all imagine the sort of man that would
be chosen? Have we no experience of what the people
love? Comrades, dear democratic ladies and gentleman,
pursue, by all means, your schemes for righting the world,
dream your dreams, conceive Utopias, but leave the artists

out. For, tell me honestly, does any one of you believe that during the last three hundred years a single good artist would have been supported by your system? And remember, unless it had supported him it would not have allowed him to exist. Remember, too, that you will have to select or reject your artists while yet they are students—you will not be able to wait until a name has been imposed on you by years of reputation with a few good judges. If Degas is now reverenced as a master that is because his pictures fetch long prices, and his pictures fetch long prices because a handful of people who would soon have been put under the great civic pump have been for years proclaiming his mastery. And during those long years how has Degas lived? On the bounty of the people who love all things beautiful, or on the intelligence and discrimination of a few rich or richish patrons? In the great State you will not be able to take your masters ready-made with years of reputation behind them; you will have to pick them yourselves, and pick them young.

Here you are, then, at the door of your annual exhibition of students' work; you are come to choose two State pensioners, and pack the rest off to clean the drains of Melbourne. They will be chosen by popular vote—the only fair way of inducting a public entertainer to a snug billet. But, unknown to you, I have placed amongst the exhibits two drawings by Claude and one by Ingres; and at this exhibition there are no names on the catalogue. Do you think my men will get a single vote? Possibly; but dare one of you suggest that in competition with any rubbishy sensation-monger either of them will stand a chance? "Oh, but," you say, "in the great new State everyone will be well educated." "Let them," I reply, "be as well educated as the M.A.s of Oxford and Cambridge who have been educated from six to six-and-twenty: and I suggest that to do even that will come pretty dear. Well, then, submit your anonymous collection of pictures to people qualified to elect members of parliament for our two ancient universities, and you know perfectly well that you will get no better result. So, don't be silly: even private patronage is less fatal to art than public. Whatever else you may get, you will never get an artist by popular election."

You say that the State will select through two or three highly sensitive officials. In the first place you have got to catch your officials. And remember, these, too, in the eyes of their fellow-workers, will be men who have got hold of a soft thing. The considerations that govern the selection of State-paid artists will control the election of State-paid experts. By what sign shall the public recognise the man of sensibility, always supposing that it is a man of sensibility the public wants? John Jones, the broker's man, thinks himself quite as good a judge of art as Mr. Fry, and apparently Mr. Asquith thinks the trustees of the National Gallery better than either. Suppose you have by some miracle laid hands on a man of aesthetic sensibility and made him your officer, he will still have to answer for his purchases to a popularly elected parliament. Things are bad enough at present: the people will not tolerate a public monument that is a work of art, neither do their obedient servants wish to impose such a thing on them; but when no one can live as an artist without becoming a public servant, when all works of art are public monuments, do you seriously expect to have any art at all? When the appointment of artists becomes a piece of party patronage does anyone doubt that a score of qualifications will stand an applicant in better stead than that of being an artist? Imagine Mr. Lloyd George nominating Mr. Roger Fry Government selector of State-paid artists. Imagine—and here I am making no heavy demand on your powers—imagine Mr. Fry appointing some obscure and shocking student of unconventional talent. Imagine Mr. Lloyd George going down to Lime-house to defend the appointment before thousands of voters, most of whom have a son, a brother, a cousin, a friend, or a little dog who, they feel sure, is much better equipped for the job.

If the great communistic society is bent on producing art—and the society that does not produce live art is damned—there is one thing, and one only, that it can do.

Guarantee to every citizen, whether he works or whether he loafs, a bare minimum of existence—say sixpence a day and a bed in the common dosshouse. Let the artist be a beggar living on public charity. Give to the industrious practical workers the sort of things they like, big salaries, short hours, social consideration, expensive pleasures. Let the artist have just enough to eat, and the tools of his trade: ask nothing of him. Materially make the life of the artist sufficiently miserable to be unattractive, and no one will take to art save those in whom the divine daemon is absolute. For all let there be a choice between a life of dignified, highly-paid, and not over-exacting employment and the despicable life of a vagrant. There can be little doubt about the choice of most, and none about that of a real artist. Art and Religion are very much alike, and in the East, where they understand these things, there has always been a notion that religion should be an amateur affair. The pungis of India are beggars. Let artists all over the world be beggars too. Art and Religion are not professions: they are not occupations for which men can be paid. The artist and the saint do what they have to do, not to make a living, but in obedience to some mysterious necessity. They do not produce to live—they live to produce. There is no place for them in a social system based on the theory that what men desire is prolonged and pleasant existence. You cannot fit them into the machine, you must make them extraneous to it. You must make pariahs of them, since they are not a part of society but the salt of the earth.

In saying that the mass of mankind will never be capable of making delicate aesthetic judgments, I have said no more than the obvious truth. A sure sensibility in visual art is at least as rare as a good ear for music. No one imagines that all are equally capable of judging music, or that a perfect ear can be acquired by study: only fools imagine that the power of nice discrimination in other arts is not a peculiar gift. Nevertheless there is no reason why the vast majority should not become very much more sensitive to art than it is; the ear can be trained to a point. But for the better appreciation, as for the freer creation, of art more liberty is needed. Ninety-nine out of every hundred people who visit picture galleries need to be delivered from that "museum atmosphere" which envelops works of art and asphyxiates beholders. They, the ninety-nine, should be encouraged to approach works of art courageously and to judge them on their merits. Often they are more sensitive to form and colour than they suppose. I have seen people show a nice taste in cottons and calicoes, and things not recognised as "Art" by the custodians of museums, who would not hesitate to assert of any picture by Andrea del Sarto that it must be more beautiful than any picture by a child or a savage. In dealing with objects that are not expected to imitate natural forms or to resemble standard masterpieces they give free rein to their native sensibility. It is only in the presence of a catalogue that complete inhibition sets in. Traditional reverence is what lies heaviest on spectators and creators, and museums are too apt to become conventicles of tradition.

Society can do something for itself and for art by blowing out of the museums and galleries the dust of erudition and the stale incense of hero-worship. Let us try to remember that art is not something to be come at by dint of study; let us try to think of it as something to be enjoyed as one enjoys being in love. The first thing to be done is to free the aesthetic emotions from the tyranny of erudition. I was sitting once behind the driver of an old horse-omnibus when a string of sandwich-men crossed us carrying "The Empire" poster. The name of Genée was on the bill. "Some call that art," said the driver, turning to me, "but we know better" (my longish hair, I surmise, discovered a fellow connoisseur): "if you want art you must go for it to the museums." How this pernicious nonsense is to be knocked out of people's heads I cannot guess. It has been knocked in so solemnly and for so long by the schoolmasters and the newspapers, by cheap textbooks and profound historians, by district visitors and cabinet ministers, by clergymen and secularists, by labour leaders, teetotallers, anti-gamblers, and public benefactors of every sort, that I am sure it will need a brighter and braver word than mine to knock it out again. But out it has to be knocked before we can have any general sensibility to art; for, while it remains, to ninety-nine out of every hundred a work of art will be dead the moment it enters a public gallery.

The museums and galleries terrify us. We are crushed by the tacit admonition frowned from every corner that these treasures are displayed for study and improvement, by no means to provoke emotion. Think of Italy—every town with its public collection; think of the religious sight-seers! How are we to persuade these middle-class masses, so patient and so pathetic in their quest, that really they could get some pleasure from the pictures if only they did not know, and did not care to know, who painted them. They cannot all be insensitive to form and colour; and if only they were not in a flutter to know, or not to forget, who painted the pictures, when they were painted, and what they represent, they might find in them the key that unlocks a world in the existence of which they are, at present, unable to believe. And the millions who stay at home, how are they to be persuaded that the thrill provoked by a locomotive or a gasometer is the real thing?—when will they understand that the iron buildings put up by Mr. Humphrey are far more likely to be works of art than anything they will see at the summer exhibition of the Royal Academy? [1] Can we persuade the travelling classes that an ordinarily sensitive human being has a better chance of appreciating an Italian primitive than an expert hagiographer? Will they understand that, as a rule, the last to feel aesthetic emotion is the historian of art? Can we induce the multitude to seek in art, not edification, but exaltation? Can we make them unashamed of the emotion they feel for the fine lines of a warehouse or a railway

[1] An example of this was the temporary police-court set up recently in Francis Street, just off the Tottenham Court Road. I do not know whether it yet stands; if so, it is one of the few tolerable pieces of modern architecture in London.

bridge? If we can do this we shall have freed works of art from the museum atmosphere; and this is just what we have got to do. We must make people understand that forms can be significant without resembling Gothic cathedrals or Greek temples, and that art is the creation, not the imitation, of form. Then, but not till then, can they go with impunity to seek aesthetic emotion in museums and galleries.

It is argued with plausibility that a sensitive people would have no use for museums. It is said that to go in search of aesthetic emotion is wrong, that art should be a part of life—something like the evening papers or the shop windows that people enjoy as they go about their business. But, if the state of mind of one who enters a gallery in search of aesthetic emotion is necessarily unsatisfactory, so is the state of one who sits down to read poetry. The lover of poetry shuts the door of his chamber and takes down a volume of Milton with the deliberate intention of getting himself out of one world and into another. The poetry of Milton is not a part of daily life, though for some it makes daily life supportable. The value of the greatest art consists not in its power of becoming a part of common existence but in its power of taking us out of it. I think it was William Morris who said that poetry should be something that a man could invent and sing to his fellows as he worked at the loom. Too much of what Morris wrote may well have been so invented. But to create and to appreciate the greatest art the most absolute abstraction from the affairs of life is essential. And as, throughout the ages, men and women have gone to temples and churches in search of an ecstasy incompatible with and remote from the preoccupations and activities of laborious humanity, so they may go to the temples of art to experience, a little out of this world, emotions that are of another. It is not as sanctuaries from life—sanctuaries devoted to the cult of aesthetic emotion—but as class-rooms, laboratories, homes of research and warehouses of tradition, that museums and galleries become noxious.

Human sensibility must be freed from the dust of erudition and the weight of tradition; it must also be freed from the oppression of culture. For, of all the enemies of art, culture is perhaps the most dangerous, because the least obvious. By "culture" it is, of course, possible to mean something altogether blameless. It may mean an education that aims at nothing but sharpening sensibility and strengthening the power of self-expression. But culture of that sort is not for sale: to some it comes from solitary contemplation, to others from contact with life; in either case it comes only to those who are capable of using it. Common culture, on the other hand, is bought and sold in open market. Cultivated society, in the ordinary sense of the word, is a congeries of persons who have been educated to appreciate *le beau et le bien*. A cultivated person is one on whom art has not impressed itself, but on whom it has been impressed—one who has not been overwhelmed by the significance of art, but who knows that the nicest people have a peculiar regard for it. The characteristic of this Society is that, though it takes an interest in art, it does not take art seriously. Art for it is not a necessity, but an amenity. Art is not something that one might meet and be overwhelmed by between the pages of *Bradshaw*, but something to be sought and saluted at appropriate times in appointed places. Culture feels no imperative craving for art such as one feels for tobacco; rather it thinks of art as something to be taken in polite and pleasant doses, as one likes to take the society of one's less interesting acquaintances. Patronage of the Arts is to the cultivated classes what religious practice is to the lower-middle, the homage that matter pays to spirit, or, amongst the better sort, that intellect pays to emotion. Neither the cultivated nor the pious are genuinely sensitive to the tremendous emotions of art and religion; but both know what they are expected to feel, and when they ought to feel it.

Now if culture did nothing worse than create a class of well-educated ladies and gentlemen who read books, attend concerts, travel in Italy, and talk a good deal about art without ever guessing what manner of thing it is, culture would be nothing to make a fuss about. Unfortunately, culture is an active disease which causes positive ill and baulks potential good. In the first place, cultivated people always wish to cultivate others. Cultivated parents cultivate their children; thousands of wretched little creatures are daily being taught to love the beautiful. If they happen to have been born insensitive this is of no great consequence, but it is misery to think of those who have had real sensibilities ruined by conscientious parents: it is so hard to feel a genuine personal emotion for what one has been brought up to admire. Yet if children are to grow up into acceptable members of the cultivated class they must be taught to hold the right opinions—they must recognise the standards. Standards of taste are the essence of culture. That is why the cultured have ever been defenders of the antique. There grows up in the art of the past a traditional classification under standard masterpieces by means of which even those who have no native sensibility can discriminate between works of art. That is just what culture wants; so it insists on the veneration of standards and frowns on anything that cannot be justified by reference to them. That is the serious charge against culture. A person familiar with the masterpieces of Europe, but insensitive to that which makes them masterpieces, will be utterly nonplussed by a novel manifestation of the mysterious "that." It is well that old masters should be respected; it were better that vital art should be welcome. Vital art is a necessity, and vital art is stifled by culture, which insists that artists shall respect the standards, or, to put it bluntly, shall imitate old masters.

The cultured, therefore, who expect in every picture at least some reference to a familiar masterpiece, create, unconsciously enough, a thoroughly unwholesome atmosphere. For they are rich and patronising and liberal. They are the very innocent but natural enemies of originality, for an original work is the touchstone that exposes educated taste masquerading as sensibility. Besides, it is reasonable that those who have been at such pains to sympathise with artists should expect artists to think and feel as they do. Originality, however, thinks and feels for itself; commonly the original artist does not live the refined, intellectual life that would befit the fancy-man of the cultured classes. He is not picturesque; perhaps he is positively inartistic; he is neither a gentleman nor a blackguard; culture is angry and incredulous. Here is one who spends his working hours creating something that seems strange and disquieting and ugly, and devotes his leisure to simple animalities; surely one so utterly unlike ourselves cannot be an artist? So culture attacks and sometimes ruins him. If he survives, culture has to adopt him. He becomes part of the tradition, a standard, a stick with which to beat the next original genius who dares to shove an unsponsored nose above water.

In the nineteenth century cultured people were amazed to find that such cads as Keats and Burns were also great poets. They had to be accepted, and their caddishness had to be explained away. The shocking intemperance of Burns was deplored in a paragraph, and passed over—as though Burns were not as essentially a drunkard as a poet! The vulgarity of Keats's letters to Fanny Brawne did not escape the nice censure of Matthew Arnold who could not be expected to see that a man incapable of writing such letters would not have written "The Eve of St. Agnes." In our day culture having failed to suppress Mr. Augustus John welcomes him with undiscriminating enthusiasm some ten years behind the times. Here and there, a man of power may force the door, but culture never loves originality until it has lost the appearance of originality. The original genius is ill to live with until he is dead. Culture will not live with him; it takes as lover the artificer of the *faux-bon*. It adores the man who is clever enough to imitate, not any particular work of art, but art itself. It adores the man who gives in an unexpected way just what it has been taught to expect. It wants, not art, but something so much like art that it can feel the sort of emotions it would be nice to feel for art. To be frank, cultivated people are no fonder of art than the Philistines; but they like to get thrills, and they like to see old faces under new bonnets. They admire Mr. Lavery's seductive banalities and the literary and erudite novelettes of M. Rostand. They go silly over Reinhardt and Bakst. These confectioners seem to give the distinction of art to the natural thoughts and feelings of cultivated people. Culture is far more dangerous than Philistinism because it is more intelligent and more pliant. It has a specious air of being on the side of the artist. It has the charm of its acquired taste, and it can corrupt because it can speak with an authority unknown in Philistia. Because it pretends to care about art, artists are not indifferent to its judgments. Culture imposes on people who would snap their fingers at vulgarity. With culture itself, even in the low sense in which I have been using the word, we need not pick a quarrel, but we must try to free the artist and the public too from the influence of cultivated opinion. The liberation will not be complete until those who have already learned to despise the opinion of the lower middle-classes learn also to neglect the standards and the disapproval of people who are forced by their emotional limitations to regard art as an elegant amenity.

If you would have fine art and fine appreciation of art, you must have a fine free life for your artists and for yourselves. That is another thing that Society can do for art: it can kill the middle-class ideal. Was ever ideal so vulnerable? The industrious apprentice who by slow pettifogging hardness works his way to the dignity of material prosperity, Dick Whittington, what a hero for a high-spirited nation! What dreams our old men dream, what visions float into the minds of our seers! Eight hours of intelligent production, eight hours of thoughtful recreation, eight hours of refreshing sleep for all! What a vision to dangle before the eyes of a hungry people! If it is great art and fine life that you want, you must renounce this religion of safe mediocrity. Comfort is the enemy; luxury is merely the bugbear of the bourgeoisie. No soul was ever ruined by extravagance or even by debauch; it is the steady, punctual gnawing of comfort that destroys. That is the triumph of matter over mind; that is the last tyranny. For how are they better than slaves who must stop their work because it is time for luncheon, must break up a conversation to dress for dinner, must leave on the doorstep the friend they have not seen for years so as not to miss the customary train?

Society can do something for art, because it can increase liberty, and in a liberal atmosphere art thrives. Even politicians can do something. They can repeal censorious laws and abolish restrictions on freedom of thought and speech and conduct. They can protect minorities. They can defend originality from the hatred of the mediocre mob. They can make an end of the doctrine that the State has a right to crush unpopular opinions in the interests of public order. A mighty liberty to be allowed to speak acceptable words to the rabble! The least that the State can do is to protect people who have something to say that may cause a riot. What will not cause a riot is probably not worth saying. At present, to agitate for an increase of liberty is the best that any ordinary person can do for the advancement of art.

2. ART AND SOCIETY

WHAT might Art do for Society? Leaven it; perhaps even redeem it: for Society needs redemption. Towards the end of the nineteenth century life seemed to be losing its savour. The world had grown grey and anæmic, lacking passion, it seemed. Sedateness became fashionable; only dull people cared to be thought spiritual. At its best the late nineteenth century reminds one of a sentimental farce, at its worst of a heartless joke. But, as we have seen, before the turn, first in France, then throughout Europe, a new emotional movement began to manifest itself. This movement if it was not to be lost required a channel along which it might flow to some purpose. In the Middle Ages such a channel would have been ready to hand; spiritual ferment used to express itself through the Christian Church, generally in the teeth of official opposition. A modern movement of any depth cannot so express itself. Whatever the reasons may be, the fact is certain. The principal reason, I believe, is that the minds of modern men and women can find no satisfaction in dogmatic religion; and Christianity, by a deplorable mischance, has been unwilling to relinguish dogmas that are utterly irrelevant to its essence. It is the entanglement of religion in dogma that still keeps the world superficially irreligious. Now, though no religion can escape the binding weeds of dogma, there is one that throws them off more easily and light-heartedly than any other. That religion is art; for art is a religion. It is an expression of and a means to states of mind as holy as any that men are capable of experiencing; and it is towards art that modern minds turn, not only for the most perfect expression of transcendent emotion, but for an inspiration by which to live.

From the beginning art has existed as a religion con-

current with all other religions. Obviously there can be
no essential antagonism between it and them. Genuine art
and genuine religion are different manifestations of one
spirit; so are sham art and sham religion. For thousands
of years men have expressed in art their ultra-human emotions, and have found in it that food by which the spirit
lives. Art is the most universal and the most permanent
of all forms of religious expression, because the significance
of formal combinations can be appreciated as well by one
race and one age as by another, and because that significance is as independent as mathematical truth of human
vicissitudes. On the whole, no other vehicle of emotion
and no other means to ecstasy has served man so well.
In art any flood of spiritual exaltation finds a channel
ready to nurse and lead it: and when art fails it is for
lack of emotion, not for lack of formal adaptability. There
never was a religion so adaptable and catholic as art. And
now that the young movement begins to cast about for
a home in which to preserve itself and live, what more
natural than that it should turn to the one religion of un-
limited forms and frequent revolutions?

For art is the one religion that is always shaping its form
to fit the spirit, the one religion that will never for long
be fettered in dogmas. It is a religion without a priesthood;
and it is well that the new spirit should not be committed
to the hands of priests. The new spirit is in the hands of
the artists; that is well. Artists, as a rule, are the last to
organise themselves into official castes, and such castes,
when organised, rarely impose on the choicer spirits. Rebellious painters are a good deal commoner than rebellious
clergymen. On compromise which is the bane of all religion—since men cannot serve two masters—almost all
the sects of Europe live and grow fat. Artists have been
more willing to go lean. By compromise the priests have
succeeded marvellously in keeping their vessel intact. The
fine contempt for the vessel manifested by the original
artists of each new movement is almost as salutary as
their sublime belief in the spirit. To us, looking at the
history of art, the periods of abjection and compromise

may appear unconscionably long, but by comparison with those of other religions they are surprisingly short. Sooner or later a true artist arises, and often by his unaided strength succeeds in so reshaping the vessel that it shall contain perfectly the spirit.

Religion which is an affair of emotional conviction should have nothing to do with intellectual beliefs. We have an emotional conviction that some things are better than others, that some states of mind are good and that others are not; we have a strong emotional conviction that a good world ought to be preferred to a bad; but there is no proving these things. Few things of importance can be proved; important things have to be felt and expressed. That is why people with things of importance to say tend to write poems rather than moral treatises. I make my critics a present of that stick. The original sin of dogmatists is that they are not content to feel and express but must needs invent an intellectual concept to stand target for their emotion. From the nature of their emotions they infer an object the existence of which they find themselves obliged to prove by an elaborately disingenuous metaphysic. The consequence is inevitable; religion comes to mean, not the feeling of an emotion, but adherence to a creed. Instead of being a matter of emotional conviction it becomes a matter of intellectual propositions. And here, very properly, the sceptic steps in and riddles the *ad hoc* metaphysic of the dogmatist with unanswerable objections. No Cambridge Rationalist can presume to deny that I feel a certain emotion, but the moment I attempt to prove the existence of its object I lay myself open to a bad four hours.

No one, however, wishes to deny the existence of the immediate object of aesthetic emotion—combinations of lines and colours. For my suggestion that there may be a remote object I shall probably get into trouble. But if my metaphysical notions are demolished in a paragraph, that will not matter in the least. No metaphysical notions about art matter. All that matter are the aesthetic emotion and its immediate object. As to the existence of a remote object and its possible nature there have been innumerable theories, most, if not all, of which have been discredited. Though a few have been defended fiercely, they have never been allowed to squeeze out art completely: dogma has never succeeded in ousting religion. It has been realised always to some extent that the significance of art depends chiefly on the emotion it provokes, that works are more important than theories. Although attempts have been made to impose dogmas, to define the remote object and to direct the emotion, a single original artist has generally been strong enough to wreck the spurious orthodoxy. Dimly it has always been perceived that a picture which moves aesthetically cannot be wrong; and that the theory that condemns it as heretical condemns itself. Art remains an undogmatic religion. You are invited to feel an emotion, not to acquiesce in a theory.

Art, then, may satisfy the religious need of an age grown too acute for dogmatic religion, but to do so art must enlarge its sphere of influence. There must be more popular art, more of that art which is unimportant to the universe but important to the individual: for art can be second-rate yet genuine. Also, art must become less exclusively professional. That will not be achieved by bribing the best artists to debase themselves, but by enabling everyone to create such art as he can. It is probable that most are capable of expressing themselves, to some extent, in form; it is certain that in so doing they can find an extraordinary happiness. Those who have absolutely nothing to express and absolutely no power of expression are God's failures; they should be kindly treated along with the hopelessly idiotic and the hydrocephalous. Of the majority it is certainly true that they have some vague but profound emotions, also it is certain that only in formal expression can they realise them. To caper and shout is to express oneself, yet is it comfortless; but introduce the idea of formality, and in dance and song you may find satisfying delight. Form is the talisman. By form the vague, uneasy, and unearthly emotions are transmuted into something definite, logical, and above the earth. Making useful objects is dreary work, but making them according to the mysterious laws of formal expression is half way to happiness. If art is to do the work of religion, it must somehow be brought within reach of the people who need religion, and an obvious means of achieving this is to introduce into useful work the thrill of creation.

But, after all, useful work must remain, for the most part, mechanical; and if the useful workers want to express themselves as completely as possible, they must do so in their leisure. There are two kinds of formal expression open to all—dancing and singing. Certainly it is in dance and song that ordinary people come nearest to the joy of creation. In no age can there be more than a few first-rate artists, but in any there might be millions of genuine ones; and once it is understood that art which is unfit for public exhibition may yet be created for private pleasure no one will feel shame at being called an amateur. We shall not have to pretend that all our friends are great artists, because they will make no such pretence themselves. In the great State they will not be of the company of divine beggars. They will be amateurs who consciously use art as a means to emotional beatitude; they will not be artists who, consciously or unconsciously, use everything as a means to art. Let us dance and sing, then, for dancing and singing are true arts, useless materially, valuable only for their aesthetic significance. Above all, let us dance and devise dances—dancing is a very pure art, a creation of abstract form; and if we are to find in art emotional satisfaction, it is essential that we shall become creators of form. We must not be content to contemplate merely; we must create; we must be active in our dealings with art.

It is here that I shall fall foul of certain excellent men and women who are attempting to "bring art into the lives of the people" by dragging parties of school children and factory girls through the National Gallery and the British Museum. Who is not familiar with those little flocks of victims clattering and shuffling through the galleries, inspissating the gloom of the museum atmosphere? What is being done to their native sensibilities by the

earnest bear-leader with his (or her) catalogue of dates
and names and appropriate comments? What have all these
tags of mythology and history, these pedagogic raptures and
peripatetic ecstasies, to do with genuine emotion? In the
guise of what grisly and incomprehensible charlatan is art
being presented to the people? The only possible effect of
personally conducted visits must be to confirm the victims
in their suspicion that art is something infinitely remote,
infinitely venerable, and infinitely dreary. They come away
with a respectful but permanent horror of that old sphinx
who sits in Trafalgar Square propounding riddles that are
not worth answering, tended by the cultured and nourished
by the rich.

First learn to walk, then try running. An artisan of exceptional sensibility may get something from the masterpieces of the National Gallery, provided there is no
cultivated person at hand to tell him what to feel, or to
prevent him feeling anything by telling him to think. An
artisan of ordinary sensibility had far better keep away
until, by trying to express himself in form, he has gained
some glimmer of a notion of what artists are driving at.
Surely there can be no reason why almost every man
and woman should not be a bit of an artist since almost
every child is. In most children a sense of form is dis-
cernible. What becomes of it? It is the old story: the child
is father to the man; and if you wish to preserve for the
man the gift with which he was born, you must catch him
young, or rather prevent his being caught. Can we by any
means thwart the parents, the teachers, and the systems
of education that turn children into modern men and
women? Can we save the artist that is in almost every
child? At least we can offer some practical advice. Do not
tamper with that direct emotional reaction to things which
is the genius of children. Do not destroy their sense of
reality by teaching them to manipulate labels. Do not
imagine that adults must be the best judges of what is
good and what matters. Don't be such an ass as to suppose
that what excites uncle is more exciting than what excites
Tommy. Don't suppose that a ton of experience is worth

a flash of insight, and don't forget that a knowledge of life can help no one to an understanding of art. Therefore do not educate children to be anything or to feel anything; put them in the way of finding out what they want and what they are. So much in general. In particular I would say, do not take children to galleries and museums; still less, of course, send them to art schools to be taught high-toned commercialism. Do not encourage them to join guilds of art and crafts, where, though they may learn a craft, they will lose their sense of art. In those respectable institutions reigns a high conception of sound work and honest workmanship. Alas! why cannot people who set themselves to be sound and honest remember that there are other things in life? The honest craftsmen of the guilds have an ideal which is praiseworthy and practical, which is mediocre and unmagnanimous, which is moral and not artistic. Craftsmen are men of principle, and, like all men of principle, they abandon the habit of thinking and feeling because they find it easier to ask and answer the question, "Does this square with my principles?"—than to ask and answer the question, "Do I feel this to be good or true or beautiful?" Therefore, I say, do not encourage a child to take up with the Arts and Crafts. Art is not based on craft, but on sensibility; it does not live by honest labour, but by inspiration. It is not to be taught in workshops and schoolrooms by craftsmen and pedants, though it may be ripened in studios by masters who are artists. A good craftsman the boy must become if he is to be a good artist; but let him teach himself the tricks of his trade by experiment, not in craft, but in art.

To those who busy themselves about bringing art into the lives of the people, I would also say—Do not dabble in revivals. The very word smacks of the vault. Revivals look back; art is concerned with the present. People will not be tempted to create by being taught to imitate. Except that they are charming, revivals of morris-dancing and folk-singing are little better than Arts and Crafts in the open. The dust of the museum is upon them. They may turn boys and girls into nimble virtuosi; they will not make them artists. Because no two ages express their sense of form in precisely the same way all attempts to recreate the forms of another age must sacrifice emotional expression to imitative address. Old-world merry-making can no more satisfy sharp spiritual hunger than careful craftsmanship or half hours with our "Art Treasures." Passionate creation and ecstatic contemplation, these alone will satisfy men in search of a religion.

I believe it is possible, though extremely difficult, to give people both—if they really want them. Only, I am sure that, for most, creation must precede contemplation. In Monsieur Poiret's *Ecole Martine* [1] scores of young French girls, picked up from the gutter or thereabouts, are at this moment creating forms of surprising charm and originality. That they find delight in their work is not disputed. They copy no master, they follow no tradition; what they owe to the past—and it is much—they have borrowed quite unconsciously with the quality of their bodies and their minds from the history and traditional culture of their race. Their art differs from savage art as a French *midinette* differs from a squaw, but it is as original and vital as the work of savages. It is not great art, it is not profoundly significant, it is often frankly third-rate, but it is genuine; and therefore I rate the artisans of the *Ecole Martine* with the best contemporary painters, not as artists, but as manifestations of the movement.

I am no devout lover of rag-time and turkey-trotting, but they too are manifestations. In those queer exasperated rhythms I find greater promise of a popular art than in revivals of folk-song and morris-dancing. At least they bear some relationship to the emotions of those who sing and dance them. In so far as they are significant they are good, but they are of no great significance. It is not in the souls of bunny-huggers that the new ferment is potent; they will not dance and sing the world out of its lethargy; not to them will the future owe that debt which I trust

[1] We may hope much from the Omega Workshops in London; but at present they employ only trained artists. We have yet to see what effect they will have on the untrained.

it will be quick to forget. There is nothing very wonderful or very novel about rag-time or tango, but to overlook any live form of expression is a mistake, and to attack it is sheer silliness. Tango and rag-time are kites sped by the breeze that fills the great sails of visual art. Not every man can keep a cutter, but every boy can buy a kite. In an age that is seeking new forms in which to express that emotion which can be expressed satisfactorily in form alone, the wise will look hopefully at any kind of dancing or singing that is at once unconventional and popular.

So, let the people try to create form for themselves. Probably they will make a mess of it; that will not matter. The important thing is to have live art and live sensibility; the copious production of bad art is a waste of time, but, so long as it is not encouraged to the detriment of good, nothing worse. Let everyone make himself an amateur, and lose the notion that art is something that lives in the museums understood by the learned alone. By practising an art it is possible that people will acquire sensibility; if they acquire the sensibility to appreciate, even to some extent, the greatest art they will have found the new religion for which they have been looking. I do not dream of anything that would burden or lighten the catalogues of ecclesiastical historians. But if it be true that modern men can find little comfort in dogmatic religion, and if it be true that this age, in reaction from the materialism of the nineteenth century, is becoming conscious of its spiritual need and longs for satisfaction, then it seems reasonable to advise them to seek in art what they want and art can give. Art will not fail them; but it may be that the majority must always lack the sensibility that can take from art what art offers.

That will be very sad for the majority; it will not matter much to art. For those who can feel the significance of form, art can never be less than a religion. In art these find what other religious natures found and still find, I doubt not, in impassioned prayer and worship. They find that emotional confidence, that assurance of absolute good, which makes of life a momentous and harmonious whole.

Because the aesthetic emotions are outside and above life, it is possible to take refuge in them from life. He who has once lost himself in an "O Altitudo" will not be tempted to over-estimate the fussy excitements of action. He who can withdraw into the world of ecstasy will know what to think of circumstance. He who goes daily into the world of aesthetic emotion returns to the world of human affairs equipped to face it courageously and even a little contemptuously. And if by comparison with aesthetic rapture he finds most human passion trivial, he need not on that account become unsympathetic or inhuman. For practical purposes, even, it is possible that the religion of art will serve a man better than the religion of humanity. He may learn in another world to doubt the extreme importance of this, but if that doubt dims his enthusiasm for some things that are truly excellent it will dispel his illusions about many that are not. What he loses in philanthropy he may gain in magnanimity; and because his religion does not begin with an injunction to love all men, it will not end, perhaps, in persuading him to hate most of them.

THE END